Executive Abundance

Leading Through Cycles of Scarcity and Success

Dr. Mitchell Levy

First Printing: May 2026
Hardcover ISBN: 978-1-60005-292-7 (1-60005-292-4)
Place of Publication: Silicon Valley, CA
Paperback Library of Congress Number: 2025922497

Trademarks

All terms mentioned in this book that are known to be trademarks or service marks have been appropriately capitalized. Neither Happy About, nor any of its imprints, can attest to the accuracy of this information. Use of a term in this book should not be regarded as affecting the validity of any trademark or service mark.

Warning and Disclaimer

Every effort has been made to make this book as complete and as accurate as possible. The information provided is on an "as is" basis. The author, publisher, and their agents assume no responsibility for errors or omissions. Nor do they assume liability or responsibility to any person or entity with respect to any loss or damages arising from the use of information contained herein.

Dedication

To every executive, entrepreneur, and purpose-driven leader who dares to dream beyond quarterly results and chooses to build a legacy rooted in trust, clarity, and authentic impact. And to my wife, whose support, patience, and love make my own Executive Abundance possible every day.

Acknowledgements

I would like to express deep gratitude to the extraordinary leaders, clients, and colleagues who have contributed to the evolution of Executive Abundance. Your honesty, challenges, and partnership have shaped these ideas and brought them to life.

I am also grateful to the more than 500 thought leaders who shared their wisdom in interviews and whose perspectives made this framework richer, more credible, and more relevant.

Special thanks to Nikka Ann Alejandro who has been my thinking partner and who's helped to shape and reshape my thinking over the last decade.

I also wish to thank Rev. Dr. Kimberly Marooney, my dissertation mentor and President of Gateway University. She challenged and supported me during my Capstone Ph.D. journey, which resulted in a set of tools, including my dissertation, this book, two chatbots, and two courses, that are much better than I could have imagined.

To my global network of colleagues, mentors, and friends… thank you for believing in the mission of credibility and helping me champion a better way to lead.

Also to my family and friends who make this trip around the sun worth it each and every day.

Preface by Dr. Mitchell Levy

As the author of this framework, I've witnessed firsthand the struggles many executives face: the relentless pressure to perform, the noise of fleeting trends, and the deep desire for something more... a success that is not just about numbers, but about meaning, impact, and a legacy of true value.

The Executive Abundance™ framework was born from years of observing leaders navigate relentless performance pressure and the tension between quarterly expectations and long-term purpose. What began as conversation matured through 500 credibility interviews, more than a thousand executive clarity engagements, extensive executive coaching work, and formal doctoral research examining leadership coherence under sustained short-term performance pressure.

This book is an invitation to explore a path toward a more fulfilling and impactful form of leadership and organizational success. It's about moving beyond the conventional "rules of the game" that so often lead to burnout and hollow victories, and instead embracing principles that foster sustainable growth, deep trust, and a profound sense of purpose.

As you progress through these pages, you will find a roadmap that takes you from clarifying where you are executing on your purpose to sustaining a credible, consistent, and committed legacy. Each chapter is designed to spark reflection, inspire micro-commitments, and build a leadership style that resonates long after you leave the boardroom. Executive Abundance is not just a concept; it is a way of being, a gift to every stakeholder, and a movement ready to be amplified through you.

Contents

Foreword

When I reflect on my journey at WD-40 Company, what comes to mind isn't just quarterly performance or product innovation... it's the tribe we built. It's the sense of purpose, the clarity of why we exist, and the credibility we earned by truly living our values every single day.

That's why Executive Abundance resonates so deeply with me. Dr. Mitchell Levy has captured what I believe every modern leader must embrace: that business success isn't only about financial return. It's about being trusted, known, and liked across all five stakeholder groups. It's about creating a culture where people feel safe, seen, and inspired to grow.

At WD-40 Company, we didn't just talk about purpose. We embedded it into every decision we made, every interaction we had with each other, and every service we provided to our customers and communities. We didn't view credibility as optional. It was, and still is, our operating system. And we led with clarity. Everyone knew our "why," and that clarity became our compass.

Executive Abundance isn't a theory. It's a practical, actionable guide to lead in today's complex world. If you're ready to build a business that performs and uplifts, that delivers results and legacy, this book will give you the roadmap. Not just for your company, but for the leader you choose to be.

Mitchell has distilled decades of insight into a model that can transform how we lead, build culture, and serve. It's not always easy, but I can tell you from experience ... it's worth it.

— Garry Ridge
Chairman Emeritus, WD-40 Company
Culture Coach & Servant Leader & Best Selling Author Any Dumb-Ass Can Do It

Introduction

Beyond the Conventional: The Call for Executive Abundance

Chasing quarterly wins while ignoring long-term purpose isn't sustainable, at least for most companies. I've seen too many leaders sacrifice clarity, credibility, and connection just to hit short-term numbers, only to end up burned out or disengaged. True success isn't measured solely by shareholder value; it's felt in how well you serve all five key stakeholder groups: Family and Self, Employees, Customers, Investors, and Community. Without that balance, even the biggest financial win can feel like a hollow victory.

There is a growing hunger for a more holistic, sustainable, and durable form of achievement... a state I call Executive Abundance, or EA: a way of leading with radical clarity, unwavering credibility, and purposeful action that positively impacts all five stakeholder groups.

This book is here to redefine what success truly means. Executive Abundance is not merely about financial prosperity, though that can be a result. It is a comprehensive state where leaders and their organizations operate with profound clarity about where they execute on their purpose and with consistent credibility, achieving sustainable growth, cultivating deep stakeholder trust, and creating a lasting positive impact.

It is about "changing the rules of the game," not by finding loopholes, but by rewriting the playbook based on enduring values, strategic foresight, and authentic leadership.

The world is saturated with noise, fake experts, and followers-for-hire. In such an environment, authentic leadership and genuine organizational value become paramount.

This book introduces the Executive Abundance Framework: a strategic approach designed to help CEOs, C-Suite executives, and their companies navigate this complexity, increase their Return on Investment (ROI) through Operational Credibility, and build businesses that are not only successful but also significant.

The principles discussed herein are drawn from extensive experience, including insights from over 500 interviews with thought leaders on credibility, decades of entrepreneurship in Silicon Valley, and a deep commitment to helping leaders articulate and execute on their purpose.

The journey to Executive Abundance requires a shift from being merely "busy" (which can be the "greatest leadership lie") to being purposefully effective. It demands congruence between what is projected externally and what is practiced internally, especially "when no one's watching."

This book will guide you through the core components of the Executive Abundance Framework:

- Understanding the current crisis of credibility and the imperative for change.
- Mastering the CPoP (Customer Point of Possibilities) to achieve radical clarity.
- Embodying the 10 Credibility Values that authentic leaders must cultivate.
- Implementing Operational Credibility to align corporate, team, and individual actions with where they execute on their purpose.
- Transforming your organization to change its rules, fostering innovation, stakeholder engagement, and market leadership.
- Cultivating a legacy that extends far beyond the balance sheet, positively impacting:
    - Family and Self (the inner engine of sustainable leadership).
    - Employees (the organizational engine).
    - Customers (the external ripple).
    - Investors (the driver of authentic, sustainable growth).
    - Community (the amplifier of legacy).

This book invites you to lead differently: through clarity, credibility, consistency, and a purpose-driven commitment to all five stakeholder groups. In the chapters ahead, we will explore not only what leadership should look like, but why misalignment happens in the first place, and how it can be prevented before erosion begins. Executive Abundance isn't just about outperforming the market; it's about redefining success for a world that demands more. It's about building trust, creating impact, and leaving a legacy that truly matters. The future of leadership isn't more noise, it's more meaning. And it starts with you.

Are you ready?

Part I

The Abundance Imperative: Why Traditional Success Metrics Fall Short

In an era where trust is eroding and short-term wins leave leaders feeling empty, Part 1 sets the stage for a radical rethinking of leadership. You'll explore why credibility is collapsing, how image-driven leadership fails, and why purpose-driven, authentic influence is the only sustainable path forward. Executive Abundance emerges here as a new blueprint (grounded in clarity, credibility, consistency, and commitment) for creating a lasting, stakeholder-centered legacy.

Chapter 1: Credibility Crisis: The Invisible Force Behind It
Credibility is under siege in a world saturated with noise, false promises, and performative leadership. Chapter 1 reveals why simply "appearing" credible no longer works, and shows how authentic leaders build trust by aligning what they say with how they act, even when no one is watching. You'll discover a modern, powerful definition of credibility that sets the tone for the Executive Abundance Framework.

Chapter 2: Redefining Success: What We Reinforce Shapes What We Become
What if success meant more than quarterly numbers or a title on your door? Chapter 2 invites you to redefine success as a holistic, purpose-driven impact that reaches Family and Self, Employees, Customers, Investors, and Community. Through the lens of Executive Abundance, you'll see how true leadership creates shared prosperity, earned trust, and a legacy felt through everyone you serve.

Chapter I

Credibility Crisis: The Invisible Force Behind It

Introduction

Credibility is under siege. We're living in a world where trust is breaking down ... in institutions, leaders, and even basic facts. The marketplace is flooded with fake experts, polished façades, and influencers chasing clicks instead of truth. It's created what I call a true "crisis of credibility." This credibility crisis is not just a leadership problem; it is the reason a new model of leadership is required.

Real leadership is no longer about titles, power, or maintaining an impressive public image. It is about congruence; ensuring your actions match your words, and where you execute on your purpose is visible in everything you do, especially when no one is watching. Authentic, vulnerable, purpose-driven leaders stand out because they build trust that lasts.

In this chapter, you will explore why traditional leadership frameworks are failing, how the erosion of credibility affects every stakeholder, and what it means to embrace Executive Abundance as a leadership philosophy rooted in clarity and consistency. This crisis is not a passing trend; it is a wake-up call for a new way to lead ... one grounded in purpose expressed through consistent action and authenticity.

The Crisis of Credibility in a Transparent World

The modern business environment is characterized by an unprecedented level of transparency and interconnectedness. Technology has democratized voice, enabling ideas (and unfortunately, misinformation) to spread at lightning speed.

We're living in a time where trust is breaking down fast. Leaders, institutions, and even basic facts are under scrutiny. It's not just about fake news or shallow influencers, it's deeper than that. It's the growing disconnect between what people say and how they actually show up. The world's tired of empty promises. Stakeholders want leaders who are real, consistent, and show up with purpose in action.

Leaders who cling to the old playbook (image-driven, superficial, short-term) risk irrelevance. The stakes have never been higher for leaders to demonstrate congruence between what they say and how they actually show up, both internally and externally.

You can see the credibility crisis everywhere. Employees are disengaged, or worse, actively resisting leadership they don't trust. Customers are more skeptical than ever, worn down by years of big promises and little follow-through. And across the board, people are disillusioned. Too many companies still put profit ahead of people and purpose, and it shows.

The rise of "fake experts" and the ease of manufacturing an impressive online façade without genuine substance only deepen the problem.

When stakeholders (family members, employees, customers, investors, and communities) see a disconnect between what leaders say and what they actually do, their trust evaporates. In this environment, people are becoming far more discerning, searching for authentic leadership rooted in consistency, transparency, and a clear articulation of purpose in action. They are no longer satisfied with polished words alone; they demand leaders whose actions match their messaging, and whose values are evident, even when no one is watching.

The old definition of credibility ("the quality that makes people believe or trust you," as the Oxford Dictionary puts it) doesn't cut it anymore in a world that's always on and watching.

In my research, originally published in *Credibility Nation*, and also seen in chapter 4, I have redefined credibility (see the three pillars of credibility in Chapter 4) as the quality of being Trusted, Known, and Liked. This modern framing recognizes that trust alone is no longer sufficient. Leaders must also be known; meaning stakeholders clearly understand who they are, what they stand for, and how they serve, and are liked, which reflects authentic connection rooted in respect, empathy, and positive human values. In the social age, connection and relatability are every bit as critical as competence and reliability.

The Three Pillars of Credibility

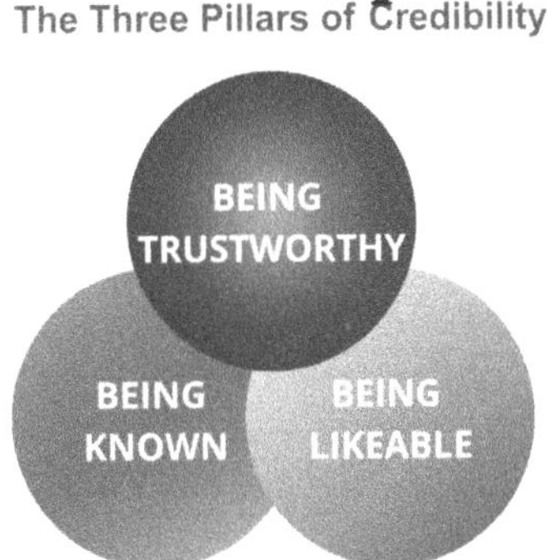

Figure 01: The Three Pillars of Credibility

This evolved definition serves as a cornerstone of the Executive Abundance Framework, empowering leaders to build enduring bonds with stakeholders through consistent, purpose-driven action.

The Invisible Force Behind the Crisis

There is another force at work in this crisis of credibility, and it rarely gets discussed openly. Measurement systems shape behavior.

What we measure becomes what we reinforce. What we reinforce becomes what we protect. And what we protect determines how leadership behaves under pressure.

In many organizations, reporting cadence has accelerated. Quarterly earnings. Monthly dashboards. Weekly metrics. Daily indicators. None of these are wrong. Financial discipline matters. Transparency matters. Accountability matters.

The challenge arises when measurement narrows. When success is defined primarily through short-term financial indicators, leadership attention narrows toward what is immediately visible and frequently reported. Over time, long-horizon decision frames compress. Cultural investments become discretionary. Development programs become deferrable. Long-horizon innovation becomes harder to defend.

Erosion rarely begins with a dramatic reversal of values. It begins with subtle reclassification. Important becomes optional. Long-horizon thinking becomes later. Purpose becomes positioning.

By the time performance reflects the shift, trust has often already thinned. This is not a failure of capitalism. It is a function of incentives.

Measurement systems create gravitational pull. Without conscious counterweights, leadership behavior will follow that pull.

This dynamic is not primarily about character. It is about structure. Incentive systems compress decision horizons. Reporting cadence narrows attention. Without intentional counterbalance, even disciplined leaders begin optimizing for what is visible in the next cycle rather than what is durable over time. Executive Abundance is designed to restore horizon.

The Demand for Authentic Leadership

The consequences of this credibility crisis are profound and far-reaching. It is not simply a matter of image management or personal integrity. It is the predictable result of systems that reward short-term visibility over long-term coherence. When credibility becomes performative rather than operational, trust erodes in ways that are difficult to reverse.

When there is a disconnect between the image projected to the outside world and the operational reality on the inside (in other words, when external integrity does not match internal integrity) the foundation of trust crumbles.

I have seen this pattern repeatedly in my research and work with thousands of executives: when the truth eventually comes out, stakeholders feel deceived, engagement collapses, and reputations suffer long-lasting damage. This is precisely why the old rules, which might have tolerated a degree of "spin" or prioritized appearance over substance, no longer apply in today's environment. The world is demanding more from its leaders, and those who refuse to evolve will be left behind.

The search for authentic leadership is a direct response to this credibility crisis. Stakeholders today are not just looking for technical competence; they are looking for leaders whose behavior remains coherent when pressure rises. They want congruence, vulnerability, and purpose that stands up to scrutiny. They want leaders who live and breathe positive human values (integrity, respect, transparency) and who use those values to build genuine trust and long-lasting relationships.

In my work and interviews with over 500 thought leaders on credibility, it is clear: the leadership crisis is not merely one of visibility, but of vulnerability and authenticity. Those leaders who choose to understand this imperative and consciously invest in building and maintaining their credibility are the ones who will thrive and guide their organizations toward an abundant future.

The alternative is stark: becoming irrelevant or, worse, joining the ranks of the "dubious" ... those who contribute to the continued erosion of humanity, trust, and empathy in our interactions.

Reflection and Action

Take time to reflect on where you stand in your own leadership journey. Ask yourself:

- Where am I showing up in a way that might feel polished on the outside but disconnected from what I truly believe?
- Is there a gap between what I say I value and what my stakeholders actually experience?
- Have I ever relied on "looking the part" instead of being the part?
- Do people around me know who I truly am, what I stand for, and how I serve?
- Where might I be unintentionally contributing to the erosion of trust: by overpromising, underdelivering, or avoiding vulnerability?

Credibility alone, however, is not the destination. It is the threshold. When credibility is lived consistently, it creates the conditions for something more sustainable and expansive to emerge. That state is what I call Executive Abundance: a way of leading where clarity, credibility, consistency, and commitment work together to create lasting value for every stakeholder you serve.

Micro-Commitment:

- ☐ Ask one colleague, one superior, and one friend if they trust you, if they feel they truly know you, and if they enjoy working with or being around you. Listen openly to their responses without defending or explaining. Let their perspective guide one small shift in how you show up with greater authenticity and alignment.

Summary

The crisis of credibility is fueled not only by a disconnect between what leaders say and what they actually do, but also by the systems that quietly reward short-term performance over long-term coherence. When leadership becomes reactive to narrow measurement, alignment erodes and trust thins. Authentic leadership is no longer optional; it is a structural necessity for sustainable influence.

Traditional definitions of credibility (limited to mere believability) no longer serve us. Instead, a modern, actionable definition is essential: credibility is the quality of being Trusted, Known, and Liked. Leaders who commit to showing up authentically, embracing vulnerability, and aligning external promises with internal practices will thrive in this new era. Those who refuse to adapt will see their influence diminish and risk becoming irrelevant.

This chapter underscores why authentic leadership is no longer optional, but a requirement for building trust, creating stakeholder value, and laying the foundation for Executive Abundance.

AHAs

- **AHA #1:** *In today's world, credibility is the currency of leadership. Without it, trust collapses.*
- **AHA #2:** *Credibility is no longer just about being believed: it's about being Trusted, Known, and Liked.*
- **AHA #3:** *Authentic leaders align what they project with how they act, even when no one is watching.*

Chapter 2

Redefining Success: What We Reinforce Shapes What We Become

Introduction

For decades, the business world has rewarded leaders who chase quarterly wins, drive profit at all costs, and play zero-sum games in highly competitive environments. These measurement systems reinforce short-term behavior, often at the expense of long-term coherence. While this approach might deliver financial results in the short term, it leaves many leaders with a hollow victory; a sense of burnout, disengagement, or disconnection from a deeper purpose. As stakeholders become more discerning and as transparency becomes the norm, traditional markers of success are proving incomplete, even toxic.

Executive Abundance represents a redefinition of what true success looks like. It reframes leadership as more than titles or power; it is about how people experience you, and how your impact radiates throughout all five stakeholder groups: Family and Self, Employees, Customers, Investors, and Community. In this model, your legacy is measured not just by numbers on a spreadsheet, but by the sustained health and alignment of the systems and people you influence.

This chapter will show how Executive Abundance offers a holistic, sustainable, and purpose-driven framework to create impact far beyond profit alone. It is a call to shift from a fragile, image-driven path toward a deeply rooted, authentic, and credible approach that leaves a meaningful legacy felt in the success of your stakeholders.

Redefining Success Through Stakeholder-Centered Abundance

Executive Abundance transcends the narrow confines of traditional business success metrics. While financial health and profitability will always be vital for a thriving enterprise, Executive Abundance proposes a broader, more sustainable, and more human-centered definition of success. It is rooted in the convergence of clarity, credibility, consistency, and commitment, driving not only durable business growth, but also profound influence and personal fulfillment for leaders. This is not a passing trend or a quick-fix strategy; it is a deeply embedded operational philosophy that reimagines how success is defined and how an organization positions itself within a broader leadership ecosystem. In this model, leaders measure success by how deeply they impact and uplift all five stakeholder groups, creating a legacy that stands the test of time.

At its heart, Executive Abundance is the "missing link between sustainable leadership, wealth, and fulfillment." It moves beyond the zero-sum mentality that often dominates competitive markets, proposing instead that true abundance is found in creating value for every stakeholder.

Figure 02: The EA Ecosystem

1. This begins with the leader's own well-being and clarity (Family and Self) because a leader who is burned out cannot sustainably serve others.
2. It extends to Employees, whose engagement and empowerment fuel the organization's internal engine.
3. From there, abundance ripples outward to Customers, whose trust and loyalty reflect authentic service.
4. Investors, in turn, benefit from sustainable results rooted in credible operations.
5. Finally, the Community feels the amplifying impact of leadership that is credible, transparent, and purpose-driven.

This holistic view recognizes that an organization behaves as a living system and its health is inseparable from the well-being and engagement of these five interconnected stakeholder groups.

Operationalizing Executive Abundance with Credibility

One of the most powerful differentiators of Executive Abundance is its emphasis on Operational Credibility. This means that a leader's stated values and purpose are not hollow statements carved into a plaque, but are expressed through the organization's decisions, operations, and culture. It is about consistency between what is promised and what is delivered, whether in how you treat employees, support customers, or engage the community.

Operational Credibility ensures that the company's words match its actions across all levels (corporate, team, and individual) creating a cohesive, purpose-driven entity that stakeholders can trust without reservation. When credibility is operationalized, it becomes a powerful, almost invisible force that sustains the organization's health and protects its reputation, even in turbulent times.

The definition of Executive Abundance appears below:

Executive Abundance Definition

A structured leadership framework in which the EA Engine of clarity, credibility, consistency, and commitment is intentionally applied across the EA Ecosystem of five interdependent stakeholder groups: family and self, employees, customers, investors, and community. Executive Abundance defines success by the sustained, trusted value created across this ecosystem through purpose in action.

Figure 03: Executive Abundance Definition

The journey toward Executive Abundance involves making several critical mindset shifts:

- **From Reactive to Purpose-Driven:** Responding to market forces without surrendering strategic direction and shaping decisions around a clearly articulated purpose and long-term vision.
- **From Superficial Image to Authentic Credibility:** Prioritizing earned credibility over manufactured perception, embracing vulnerability, and ensuring consistency between your words and your actions.

- **From Siloed Operations to Ecosystem Thinking:** Understanding that your organization is not an island, but a living part of a greater ecosystem, where sustainable success depends on building mutually beneficial relationships that strengthen the system as a whole.
- **From Short-Term Gains to Lasting Legacy:** Committing to building a positive, enduring impact, so that your leadership legacy is whispered behind your back and carried forward, rather than merely etched on a plaque.

Achieving Executive Abundance means a company is more than just profitable. It becomes a trusted partner, an employer of choice, an innovative force, and a responsible corporate citizen.

Taken together, these outcomes represent the lived expression of a company's brand. In an Executive Abundance organization, the brand is no longer a marketing promise or a positioning statement. It is how the organization behaves, how decisions are made, and how stakeholders experience the company over time. Executive Abundance does not replace brand value; it amplifies it by making trust, clarity, and credibility visible and durable.

As a result, success is amplified when it is shared, built on a foundation of integrity, clarity, and aligned purpose. This holistic approach empowers organizations to truly change the rules of the game, not by exploiting the system, but by elevating it through authentic, sustainable, stakeholder-centered leadership.

Reflection and Action

Consider these questions as you start your Executive Abundance journey:

- Where do you see a credibility gap between what you say and what you actually do?
- Which stakeholder group currently struggles most to trust your leadership?
- What small step can you take this week to reinforce credibility with that group?

Micro-Commitment:

- ☐ Ask for honest feedback from one stakeholder (a family member, an employee, a customer, an investor, or a community partner) about where you might be falling short on your promises. Listen fully, and decide on one change to close that credibility gap.

Summary

This chapter redefined success through the lens of Executive Abundance, showing why traditional metrics like profit alone are no longer sufficient. It described how authentic, purpose-driven leadership creates holistic impact across all five stakeholder groups (Family and Self, Employees, Customers, Investors, and Community) by aligning clarity, credibility, consistency, and commitment. Operational Credibility emerged as a core principle, ensuring a leader's promises are backed by consistent, transparent behaviors at every level.

Finally, this chapter laid out the critical shifts required to move from a reactive, image-driven mindset to a sustainable, stakeholder-centered legacy. By embracing Executive Abundance, leaders can change the rules of the game, not through exploitation, but through elevation and building organizations that thrive, endure, and inspire.

AHAs

- **AHA #4:** *True success is measured in the positive impact you have on all stakeholders, not just your bottom line.*
- **AHA #5:** *Executive Abundance is not a tactic, it's a philosophy of leadership rooted in clarity, credibility, consistency, and commitment.*
- **AHA #6:** *A leader's legacy is whispered behind their back, and felt in the thriving success of those they serve.*

Part 2

The EA Engine: Clarity, Credibility, Consistency, and Commitment

In Part 1, we examined the pressures shaping modern leadership and how narrowing measurement systems can quietly erode alignment. Awareness alone does not solve that problem.

Now we turn to the operating system.

Executive Abundance requires more than intention. It requires structure. The EA Engine is composed of four interdependent components: clarity, credibility, consistency, and commitment. Together, they convert purpose into durable value for stakeholders.

This is not a collection of virtues. It is a system. When one component weakens, the others distort. When they reinforce one another, alignment becomes durable across cycles of scarcity and success.

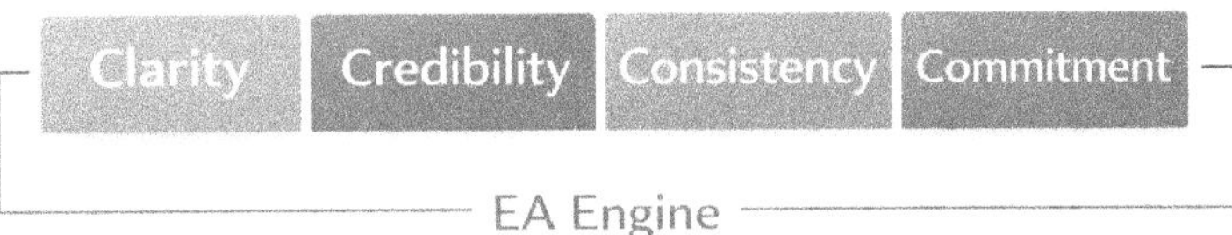

Figure 04. The EA Engine

- Clarity defines direction.
- Credibility earns belief.
- Consistency establishes reliable pattern.
- Commitment protects that pattern when short term pressure intensifies.

Chapters 3 through 6 unpack each component in depth. You will define your CPoP for radical clarity, build credibility rooted in trust, operationalize consistency into daily execution, and strengthen commitment so alignment holds when pressure rises.

If Part 1 showed why the rules must change, Part 2 provides the architecture to begin rewriting them.

What follows is not theory. It is structure you can apply.

Chapter 3: Clarity: Defining Direction Through Your CPoP
Chapter 3 guides you to craft a clear, memorable CPoP … the anchor of your Executive Abundance. You'll discover how a well-formed CPoP cuts through noise, connects you with your ideal stakeholders, and becomes the credibility compass for every strategic decision you make.

Chapter 4: Credibility: Being Trusted, Being Known, and Being Liked
In Chapter 4, you will redefine credibility beyond surface-level expertise. You'll see how trust, recognition, and genuine likability interlock to form a durable reputation that sustains Executive Abundance. This is the foundation of how leaders become the real deal, not just look the part.

Chapter 5: Consistency: Protecting Trust Through Pattern Integrity
Chapter 5 explores how trust is built through repeated alignment between words and actions. Consistency is not about rigidity; it is about pattern integrity. When leaders behave predictably across contexts and over time, credibility strengthens. You will learn how to translate values into daily decisions so that trust becomes reinforced through repetition, not intention alone.

Chapter 6: Commitment: Sustaining Priorities Under Pressure
Chapter 6 focuses on sustaining purpose when pressure intensifies. Commitment is the discipline of protecting long-term priorities even when short-term incentives pull in another direction. You will learn how to align strategies, teams, and systems so that decisions consistently reinforce your organization's purpose and its commitments to stakeholders. Operational credibility becomes the vehicle that sustains Executive Abundance across cycles of scarcity and success.

The EA Engine in Motion

In Part 2, we establish the architecture of the EA Engine.

- Clarity defines direction.
- Credibility earns belief.
- Consistency establishes reliable pattern.
- Commitment protects that pattern when short-term pressure intensifies.

Together, these four components operate as the EA Engine.

When they reinforce one another, leadership becomes durable. When one weakens, the others distort.

Chapter 3

Clarity: Defining Direction Through Your CPoP

Introduction

In a world overflowing with noise and distraction, leaders and organizations cannot afford to be vague. Clarity is not a luxury; it is structural. It shapes decisions, filters trade-offs, and determines how leadership behaves when pressure rises. Without it, even well-meaning leaders risk confusing their teams, weakening stakeholder trust, and drifting from where they execute on their purpose.

This chapter introduces the CPoP (Customer Point of Possibilities), a disciplined formula that defines where and how you execute on your purpose today. Your CPoP is a concise, memorable statement of three to nine words that communicates who you serve and what specific possibility you unlock for them. It is more than a mission statement or tagline.

Your CPoP functions as both compass and magnet. As a compass, it serves as a strategic and decision filter, guiding where you invest time, capital, and attention. As a magnet, when shared consistently, it reinforces alignment and attracts stakeholders who resonate with the value you create.

In the pages ahead, you will learn how to craft, refine, and live your CPoP, using it to guide decisions, rally teams, and sustain alignment across every stakeholder group you serve. When clarity is radical and actionable, it becomes the first component of the EA Engine, converting intention into consistent direction.

Why Clarity Matters More Than Ever

Too many leaders today are drowning in noise and distraction, and without clarity, it's almost impossible to lead with confidence and build trust. Organizations are inundated with noise from all directions: shifting market conditions, rapid technological change, information overload, and stakeholders who are more discerning and skeptical than ever. In this environment, it is easy for leaders to default to vague mission statements or half-formed strategies, hoping something will stick. But vagueness is the enemy of trust and engagement.

When clarity is missing, employees lose focus and alignment. Customers struggle to see why they should choose you or stay loyal to your brand. Stakeholders detect contradictions between what you say and what you do, eroding your credibility. Confusion spreads, trust fractures, and opportunities slip away.

When clarity is weak, pressure magnifies the drift. In moments of urgency, leaders default to what is easiest to measure or defend. Without a clear CPoP anchoring decisions, priorities shift subtly. Important becomes optional. Long-horizon thinking becomes later. Purpose becomes positioning. Erosion rarely begins with a public reversal; it begins with small inconsistencies that compound over time.

Radical clarity is the antidote. It cuts through confusion like a spotlight, making your purpose clear and magnetic. Clarity gives employees confidence in their roles and direction. It shows customers exactly what possibility you create for them and why it matters. It signals to investors, partners, and communities that you are grounded, intentional, and worthy of trust.

In a world where everyone is trying to be louder, clarity is how you stand out because people will always lean in to a leader who knows exactly where they are going and why. That is why this Part begins with clarity as the first component in the EA Engine: you cannot lead others to abundance if you cannot first articulate your own.

What Is a CPoP?

The Customer Point of Possibilities or **CPoP** is the foundation of radical clarity. It is a concise statement, 3-9 words, that captures where you are executing on your purpose today. Unlike a mission statement or a slogan, your CPoP is designed to instantly communicate who you serve and what possibility you unlock for them.

A powerful CPoP has two parts:

1. **The class of clients or audience you serve.**
2. **The specific problem, issue, or aspiration they have or want addressed.**

The Secret CPoP Formula

Your Customer Point of Possibilities (CPoP) consists of:

1. WHO you Serve.
2. WHAT Pain Point those you serve think they have or Pleasure Point they want to reach.

Figure 05: The Secret CPoP Formula

For example, instead of saying, "We help businesses grow," a strong CPoP might be "Tech Founders Scaling Stakeholder Trust," or "Business Leaders Escaping Slimy LinkedIn Sales Tactics." These statements are short, memorable, and designed to spark a "Tell me more" conversation.

The beauty of a CPoP is its clarity and shareability. It allows people inside your organization to rally behind a single, crisp expression of purpose. It also helps external audiences (customers, partners, investors, and the community) immediately understand your unique impact. In this way, the CPoP becomes both a credibility compass (guiding your decisions) and a credibility magnet (attracting aligned opportunities).

The world doesn't need another slogan. It needs leaders who can state, with clarity and courage, what possibility they are delivering right now. That's what makes the CPoP such a powerful starting point for Executive Abundance.

How to Develop Your CPoP

Defining your CPoP is not an intellectual exercise alone; it is a clarity practice that requires deep listening, reflection, and simplification. It challenges you to strip away the jargon, buzzwords, and ego-driven statements that so often clutter corporate messaging. Instead, a strong CPoP flows from authentic execution of purpose and centers on what truly matters to the people you serve.

Here are the core questions to guide you:

- **Who do you serve today?** Identify the class of clients or audience you are best equipped to help right now. If you can't pick one, look at where 80% of your revenue comes from.

- **What specific possibility do you unlock?** Think beyond "features" or "products" and focus on the transformational outcome you deliver.
- **What are they hungry for?** Consider their aspirations, not just their pain points. What do they most want to achieve or experience?
- **How do you uniquely deliver that?** What differentiates your approach, mindset, or capabilities?

One proven method is to host a **Clarity Session** (see Appendix E). This is a focused workshop (ideally with an outside facilitator if you can) where your team openly explores these questions, distills insights, and pressure-tests possible statements. The goal is to arrive at a CPoP that is memorable, inspiring, and free of corporate fluff.

Remember:

- 3-9 words.
- Easy to say and remember.
- Centered on the core problem addressed or key possibility created for the audience.
- Makes people say, "Tell me more."

When you develop your CPoP, you create a living "execution of purpose" statement. Not a static poster on a wall but a statement that energizes your leadership and clarifies your path forward.

If you'd like help creating/refining your CPoP, please go to The CPoP Architect™ GPT bot: https://aha.pub/TheCPoPArchitect. This resource is designed to guide you through the process. It will help you sharpen your statement so it resonates and passes the "Tell me more" test.

Bringing Your CPoP to Life

A powerful CPoP is only valuable if it lives beyond a strategy document or workshop flipchart. To make your CPoP real, you need to embed it in your daily operations, culture, and communications. It should become the lens through which you make decisions, rally your team, and build trust with every stakeholder.

First, share your CPoP widely. Communicate it to your team in meetings, internal newsletters, onboarding materials, and strategy sessions. Make sure everyone can explain it, believe in it, and see how their role supports it. When people across your organization align around the same clarity, collaboration accelerates and silos dissolve.

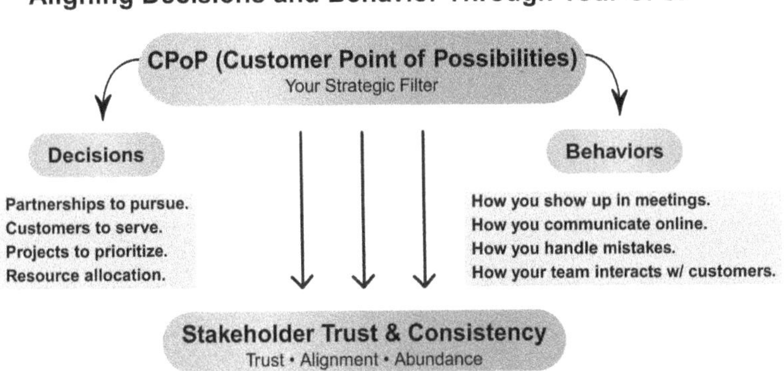

Figure 06: Aligning Decisions and Behavior Through Your CPoP

Second, use your CPoP as a strategic filter (see Figure 06). Every time you launch a new product, pursue a partnership, or design a campaign, ask: Does this advance our CPoP? If not, consider whether it fits at all. This discipline prevents mission creep and ensures that your brand promise and internal behavior stay aligned.

Third, operationalize your CPoP with rituals. For example, hosting an "Accountability Mondays" session (see Appendix F) can help teams revisit how their week's priorities serve the CPoP, identify gaps, and realign quickly. Over time, these rituals make clarity a habit, not an event.

Activating Your CPoP

Defining your CPoP is only the beginning. The real power happens when you consistently activate it. A strong CPoP should always spark curiosity, what I call the "tell me more" effect. That moment of intrigue opens the door for authentic conversation and trust.

Once you have that curiosity, share your CPoP everywhere:

- In person.
- Online.
- On your slides.
- In your emails.
- In your corporate literature.

The more consistently you repeat it, the more it becomes a **credibility magnet**. This is **Step 2 in Figure 07.** By showing up synchronously (in conversations) and asynchronously (in content), you build an unshakable foundation of trust.

EA Clarity Roadmap

Your Clarity Statement (CPoP)
01
02
Consistent Credibility (CPoPPing™)
Confidence
03
Client Magnet (CPoPPing™)
Micro-Commitment + Your Audience
04
Community Superhero (CPoPPing™)
Clients, Partners, Referral Network

Figure 07: EA Clarity Roadmap to Success

As you deploy your clarity and confidently showcase consistent credibility, you begin to attract the right audience. This allows you to hone in on creating a powerful Client Magnet, one that inspires micro-commitments from those who are aligned with the possibility you create. And when you're consistently delivering value, you naturally evolve into a Community Superhero, earning the trust and advocacy of your clients, partners, and referral network.

When you live your CPoP as a practice, you create word-of-mouth momentum. Stakeholders can clearly understand and share your message, referring you and advocating for the value you create.

That is what I call **CPoPping**™: demonstrating where you are executing on your purpose, through every choice, every conversation, every system. The more consistently you do this, the more your CPoP becomes a credibility force multiplier. See Figure 08 to see how the CPoP acts as your compass to enable CPoPping.

When your CPoP is activated in this way, it truly functions as both your compass and your magnet, clarifying your path and drawing the right opportunities toward you.

<u>A clear, lived CPoP becomes an unstoppable magnet for opportunities, loyalty, and growth … not because you pushed harder, but because you stood clearer.</u>

CPoPPing in Action (Your Playbook)

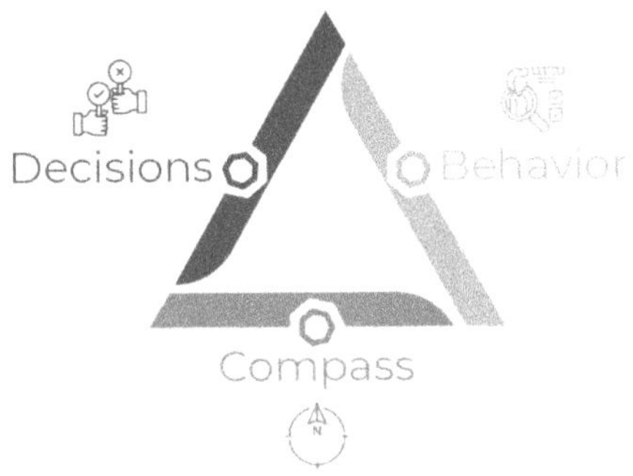

Figure 08: CPoPping in Action (Your Playbook)

Turning Your CPoP into a Magnet

At this stage, it's important to pause and reflect on how clearly your execution of purpose is communicated. Many leaders assume they are clear, but assumptions are dangerous. If you asked every person on your team to explain where the company executes on its purpose in one sentence, would they say the same thing? Would your customers instantly recognize it? Would your community feel it in how you operate?

Remember: clarity is not a one-time announcement; it is a living practice. The more you test, refine, and repeat your CPoP, the more powerful it becomes.

Reflection and Action

Use these questions to test your clarity:

- Is the execution of our purpose clear, memorable, and 3-9 words?
- Can our stakeholders (inside and outside the organization) easily explain what possibility we unlock?
- Do our daily actions and decisions reflect the CPoP we claim?
- When we share our CPoP, do referral partners and prospects lean in and say, "Tell me more"?

- Where could we share it more consistently?
- How do our decisions align with the promise of our CPoP?

If you want guided support in articulating your CPoP, some leaders use a structured reflection tool I created, The CPoP Architect™, to clarify who they serve and what truly matters. Go to https://aha.pub/TheCPoPArchitect.

Micro-Commitment:

Consider setting a micro-commitment this week:

- ☐ Host a brief team discussion to test how consistently people can state the CPoP.
- ☐ Draft a first version of your CPoP if you haven't yet, and share it with trusted advisors for feedback.
- ☐ Begin integrating the CPoP into one meeting or decision-making session to see how it shifts focus.
- ☐ Write down your CPoP and share it in three new places this week. Then watch for the reactions you receive, and adjust to make it even stronger.

Summary

Clarity is the essential first component in the EA Engine. Without it, even the best strategies and intentions falter. This chapter introduced the CPoP as a powerful tool to define and communicate where you are executing on your purpose in 3-9 words. You explored how a CPoP can act as both your credibility compass and your credibility magnet, aligning your people, decisions, and market presence around a single, powerful idea. Finally, you learned how to bring your CPoP to life through consistent action, rituals, and the practice of CPoPping™, making clarity an ongoing habit that fuels authentic credibility.

AHAs

- **AHA #7:** *Radical clarity attracts trust faster than any marketing trick.*
- **AHA #8:** *A CPoP is not what you do, it's the possibility you unlock.*
- **AHA #9:** *If your team can't explain where you're executing on your purpose in 3-9 words, they can't live it.*

Chapter 4

Credibility: Being Trusted, Being Known, and Being Liked

Introduction

If clarity is the first component of the EA Engine, then credibility is the second ... the essential element that transforms clarity of purpose into meaningful influence. Whether you are an individual leader or an entire organization, credibility is the bridge between what you promise and what people believe. It is the quality that earns you permission to lead, to inspire, to make an impact, and to sell. Without it, even the best-defined CPoP will struggle to gain traction.

Credibility can no longer rest on titles, polished messaging, or outdated authority signals. Stakeholders (from employees to customers to investors to the community) expect to see evidence that you are the real deal. They look for a consistent alignment between what you say and what you do, how you show up, and how you deliver.

This chapter explores credibility through three interlocking pillars: Being Trusted, Being Known, and Being Liked. These principles apply whether you are leading a global corporation or running your own practice. At the organizational level, credibility translates into consistent culture, reliable promises, and authentic relationships with every stakeholder group. At the individual level, it means showing up with integrity, vulnerability, and purpose in action.

When these pillars are strong, you unlock loyalty, engagement, and permission to innovate. When they are weak, you risk irrelevance or even reputational collapse. Building and maintaining credibility is not a one-time achievement; it is a living, daily practice that supports every aspect of Executive Abundance.

Why Credibility Is Non-Negotiable

With so much hype, noise, and surface-level nonsense out there, credibility is no longer a nice-to-have; it's the real currency of leadership. People have been burned too many times by overpromises, flashy branding, and "fake experts" who fail to deliver. Trust has eroded, and with it, the tolerance for leaders and organizations who cannot demonstrate authenticity and consistency in their actions.

For individuals, this means you must show that your skills, values, and purpose are not simply claims but lived commitments. For organizations, it means that culture, brand, and operations must align consistently and transparently with what you say you stand for. Customers, employees, and partners now have the tools and platforms to see through empty statements. They expect consistency, honesty, and evidence of integrity.

Credibility is the quality that earns you permission to move forward. It is what allows your audience (whether that's a team of five or a customer base of five million) to grant you their attention, loyalty, and trust. Without credibility, even a brilliant, clarity of purpose will fail because no one believes you can deliver on it.

That is why credibility is non-negotiable. It is the second component in the Executive Abundance Engine because it gives power to your clarity, transforming how you are executing on your purpose from a statement into a trusted, believable commitment. In a time when reputations can rise or collapse overnight, building authentic credibility is no longer optional . . . it is essential.

When credibility weakens, pressure accelerates exposure. Under scrutiny, misalignment becomes visible. Small compromises made for convenience begin to surface. Stakeholders sense incongruence long before metrics reflect it. Trust rarely collapses in a single moment; it thins gradually when actions and declarations drift apart.

The Three Pillars of Credibility

True credibility is far more than being believable; it is the deep, human connection that allows people to trust you, know you, and genuinely like you. These three pillars form the backbone of sustainable, stakeholder-centered leadership and apply equally to individuals and to organizations.

Being Trusted is the foundation. Trust is earned by demonstrating integrity, delivering on promises, and showing a consistency between your external presence and your internal values. Whether you are a CEO, a project manager, or an entire brand, trust grows when you practice vulnerability, admit mistakes, and stay coachable. People trust those who are willing to learn and improve, not those who pretend they have all the answers.

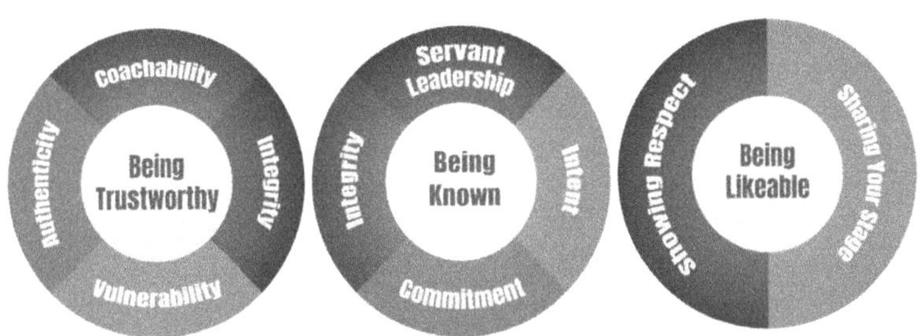

Figure 09: Dr. Mitchell Levy's Credibility Framework

Being Known builds on trust. It is not simply about recognition or visibility, but about ensuring that people genuinely understand who you are, what you stand for, and what consistent value you deliver. Being Known means stakeholders can describe where you execute on your purpose, your values, and how you serve, beyond just name recognition. It is about authentic familiarity, rooted in repeated, meaningful interactions. You earn this by publishing, speaking, mentoring, sharing your insights, and showing up generously. For organizations, it means aligning messaging, behavior, and brand presence with the clarity of your CPoP so the market sees, feels, and trusts the unique possibility you unlock.

Being Liked completes the triad. Likability is not superficial charm; it is rooted in respect, empathy, and shared humanity. People like working with, buying from, and supporting leaders and organizations who treat them with dignity, who share credit generously, and who show humility and kindness. When you "share your stage," lift others up, and act with genuine care, likability flourishes, and with it, collaboration and stakeholder goodwill.

In practice, respect shows up in small, observable ways: listening without interrupting, disagreeing without diminishing, honoring commitments even when inconvenient, and acknowledging the humanity of the person in front of you. When respect is missing, people withdraw effort long before they voice concern. When it is present, trust deepens quietly but powerfully.

These three pillars (Trusted, Known, and Liked) reinforce one another. Trust makes your message believable. Being Known ensures that people genuinely understand who you are, what you stand for, and what possibility you deliver, spreading your authentic impact. Being Liked makes others want to join you on the journey and share in your mission. Together, they create a resilient, durable form of credibility that cannot be faked and cannot be easily disrupted.

The 10 Credibility Values

Building true credibility requires more than good intentions; it takes daily practice grounded in values that people can see, feel, and experience. Through my research with Credibility Nation, interviewing over 500 thought leaders, I uncovered ten values that repeatedly show up in authentic, impactful leadership. These values are universal, applying to individuals and organizations alike, and map directly to the three pillars of credibility.

Here is a concise overview:

Pillar: Being Trusted

1. **Coachability:** demonstrating a willingness to learn, adapt, and grow.
2. **Authenticity:** showing up as your true self, on and off stage.
3. **Vulnerability:** being willing to share your humanity and your lessons.
4. **External Integrity:** the integrity you state publicly.

Pillar: Being Known

5. **Servant Leadership:** putting others first, leading through service.
6. **Intent to Do the Right Thing:** showing genuine, positive motives.
7. **Commitment to Do the Right Thing:** proving you will follow through, even when it's hard.
8. **Internal Integrity:** ensuring your private behavior matches your public statements.

Pillar: Being Liked

9. **Showing Respect:** treating people with dignity, listening deeply, and honoring their contributions.
10. **Sharing Your Stage (Credust™):** generously spotlighting and celebrating others.

These ten values are not checkboxes to occasionally revisit; they are continuous practices woven into how you lead, how you operate, and how you build relationships. When you intentionally live these values, you embody credibility from the inside out.

As you move forward, reflect on which values come naturally to you, and which might need intentional strengthening. Remember, credibility is a daily choice, and these values offer a roadmap for making that choice visible and impactful.

Embedding Credibility in Daily Practice

Credibility is not built in grand gestures alone; it is woven into the daily habits, systems, and culture that define how you operate. Whether you lead a team of five or an organization of fifty thousand people, embedding credibility means making it clear, expected, and repeatable.

For individuals, this might look like setting aside time each week to reflect on whether your words match your actions, or seeking feedforward (a practice originated by Marshall Goldsmith that focuses on future improvements rather than past mistakes) from mentors and peers about how you are showing up. For organizations, it means creating accountability systems, feedback loops, and transparent reporting practices that demonstrate you truly live your stated values.

A few powerful practices:

- **Credibility rituals:** such as "Accountability Mondays," where teams review how their actions align with the organization's CPoP and values.
- **Integrity check-ins:** quarterly or monthly reviews of decisions, communication, and outcomes, asking: *Did we do what we said we would do?*
- **Feedforward channels:** encouraging both anonymous and open feedforward from employees, customers, and partners to uncover gaps in trust.
- **Recognition systems:** rewarding credible behaviors, not just financial wins or short-term results.

These practices ensure that credibility is not just a marketing story but a lived, operational truth. They also build resilience, because credible organizations can navigate setbacks without losing the trust of their stakeholders.

Reflection and Action

Take a moment to reflect on your current credibility journey. Consider where your words and actions are fully aligned, and where they might be drifting apart. Credibility isn't something you have or don't have; it's something you demonstrate every day.

- Which of the three credibility pillars (Trusted, Known, or Liked) feels strongest for you right now? Which one needs more intentional focus?
- What credibility value comes most naturally to you? Which one have you unintentionally neglected?
- Where in your organization or leadership do you see a gap between what's promised and what's delivered?

For leaders who want help examining how they are experienced across stakeholder groups, some choose to reflect further using The Credibility Compass™, a guided framework for exploring what it means to be Trusted, Known, and Liked. Check out The Credibility Compass chatbot at https://aha.pub/TheCredibilityCompass.

Micro-Commitment

Choose one credibility value this week (perhaps **Vulnerability** or **Sharing Your Stage**) and make it visible in how you lead.

- ☐ Share a recent mistake and what you learned (Vulnerability).
- ☐ Highlight someone else's contribution in a meeting or post (Credust™).
- ☐ Ask for feedforward on how well you're living your stated values (Coachibility).

Credibility compounds through consistency. Make it a habit, not an afterthought.

Summary

Credibility is the second component in the EA Engine, converting clear execution of purpose into trustworthy influence. In this chapter, you explored the three pillars of modern credibility (being Trusted, Known, and Liked) and saw how these qualities apply to both individuals and organizations. You also discovered the ten Credibility Values that bring these pillars to life, providing a practical credibility framework to build authentic relationships and stakeholder trust. Finally, you learned how to embed credibility in daily habits, rituals, and systems, ensuring that it becomes a sustainable, operational reality rather than a one-time promise. Credibility is no longer optional; it is the backbone of a legacy that matters.

AHAs

- **AHA #10:** *Credibility gives your purpose in action permission to be heard.*
- **AHA #11:** *Trust is built in actions, not announcements.*
- **AHA #12:** *Being trusted, known, and liked is not a bonus, it is a baseline.*

Chapter 5

Consistency: Protecting Trust Through Pattern Integrity

Introduction

If clarity is where you define where you execute on your purpose, and credibility is how you demonstrate that execution in a way that earns trust and builds connection, then consistency is what makes that purpose real in practice ... day after day, action after action. Consistency is the third component in the EA Engine, transforming stated intentions into lived experiences for every stakeholder.

Inconsistent leaders and organizations confuse people. They create doubt, diminish trust, and leave stakeholders wondering which version of them will show up next. Consistency, on the other hand, signals dependability. It tells your family, employees, customers, investors, and community that your commitment is not situational but sustainable.

In this chapter, you will discover how to operationalize credibility through consistent processes, systems, and behaviors. You will see how consistency amplifies trust, protects your reputation, and supports the bold ambitions of Executive Abundance. When your actions consistently match your words, you become a credible, reliable force for positive change, and a magnet for loyalty and long-term success.

Why Consistency Builds Trust

Trust is not earned through grand gestures or powerful words alone; it is built, moment by moment, through consistent behavior. When people know what to expect from you, they feel safe to invest their time, energy, and resources. This is true for individuals and for organizations alike: consistency signals reliability, and reliability is the root of trust.

Inconsistent leaders, by contrast, undermine confidence. When words change from one conversation to the next, or actions do not align with stated values, people naturally begin to doubt. Employees hesitate to commit fully, customers question their loyalty, and investors pull back. The costs of inconsistency are enormous, creating wasted effort, stalled momentum, and reputational damage that can take years to repair.

Consistency becomes a cultural anchor. It gives teams a predictable rhythm, creates stability in times of change, and demonstrates that your values are not situational but enduring. It also builds stakeholder confidence; because when people see you deliver on your promises repeatedly, their belief in you deepens and grows.

In a distracted world hungry for genuine leadership, consistency is a competitive differentiator. It transforms your clarity and credibility from words on a slide into an operational truth that everyone can see, feel, and trust.

When consistency fractures, predictability disappears. In stable conditions, inconsistency can be masked by momentum. Under pressure, however, patterns matter. Teams begin to question priorities. Stakeholders test reliability. Without consistent reinforcement of declared values, credibility becomes episodic rather than structural.

What Is Operational Credibility?

Operational Credibility is the mechanism that takes your CPoP and values, and hardwires them into the way your organization or you as a leader actually function day to day. It is the system

The Operational Credibility Alignment Model

Purpose-Driven Organization

Aligned Teams

Purposeful Individuals

Figure 10: The Operational Credibility Alignment Model

that ensures your credibility does not live only in speeches or on mission posters, but is woven directly into decisions, processes, and behaviors.

When you build Operational Credibility, you create a culture and structure where trust is continually reinforced. It means stakeholders (family, employees, customers, partners, investors, and the community) see tangible evidence that your stated intentions and your operational realities match.

Operational Credibility functions at three essential levels:

- **Corporate Level:** ensuring that strategy, investments, and policies reflect the organization's purpose and values.
- **Team/Community Level:** building rituals, collaboration patterns, and team behaviors that align with your commitments, so everyone feels ownership in delivering on your purpose.
- **Individual Level:** empowering people to connect their daily work to the broader organizational mission, giving them permission and tools to act with integrity and accountability.

When you align these three levels, you create a unified experience where consistency becomes automatic ... not an exception, but the rule. Operational Credibility is how you turn clarity and credibility into a durable, living practice that fuels Executive Abundance.

Systems and Rituals for Consistency

Consistency is rarely accidental. It is the product of well-designed systems and intentional rituals that remind people, every day, of what matters most. These structures make it easier for leaders and organizations to stay true to where they are executing on their purpose, even under pressure.

For example, hosting a weekly ritual like Accountability Mondays (see Appendix F) can keep teams grounded. These check-ins allow people to review priorities, connect them back to the CPoP, and discuss whether current actions are aligned with stated values. This helps prevent drift and keeps your purpose visible in everyday decisions.

Other consistency-building practices include:

- **Transparent dashboards and scorecards** so everyone can see how well the organization is living its values and achieving stakeholder promises.

- **Clear role expectations** that ensure every employee understands how their work supports the organization's purpose.
- **Recognition programs** that reward credible, consistent behavior rather than just short-term performance spikes.
- **Feedforward systems** including open-door policies, surveys, and employee forums to identify where consistency might be breaking down.

These rituals and systems make credibility a daily habit, not a marketing slogan. They help build resilience, because in times of crisis, a consistent organization adapts without abandoning its core values. Ultimately, these practices transform consistency from a nice-to-have into a cultural cornerstone … one that drives long-term trust, engagement, and loyalty.

Aligning Purpose, People, and Processes

Consistency thrives when purpose, people, and processes are aligned. If even one of these elements drifts out of sync, credibility suffers and confusion takes root. That is why deliberate alignment is so critical for sustaining Executive Abundance.

Your CPoP must remain the north star. If your CPoP defines where you are executing on your purpose today; make sure that every major decision, strategic move, or market pivot stays anchored to it. When purpose in action is clear, it gives teams confidence and guards against chasing distractions that dilute trust.

People are the amplifiers of consistency. Equip your teams to live the CPoP by giving them the tools, training, and language to explain it, share it, and apply it. Reinforce their sense of ownership and help them see how their work connects directly to delivering on your stated possibility. When employees are aligned, they become powerful ambassadors of your credibility.

Processes are the backbone of consistency. Build systems, workflows, and measurement practices that make it easy for people to act with integrity and stay true to where you are executing your purpose. Whether it is a hiring process, a sales pipeline, or a project review, processes should reinforce your values not compete with them.

When purpose, people, and processes work in harmony, consistency feels effortless and organic. Stakeholders experience the same authentic values whether they interact with your front-line team, senior executives, or brand messaging. That unity builds the strongest form of trust and sets the stage for the final component in the EA Engine: commitment.

Reflection and Action

Consistency is never perfect, but it can be intentional. Taking a moment to reflect can help you spot the gaps before they turn into credibility fractures. Use these questions to guide an honest self-assessment:

- Where in our organization, or my leadership, might we say one thing but do another?
- Which processes and rituals support credible, values-driven behavior, and which might undermine it?
- Are we as consistent when no one is watching as we are when everyone is watching?
- How often do we pause to ask: Does this align with our CPoP?

Micro-Commitment:

As you answer these questions, identify one small micro-commitment you can implement this week. It might be:

- ☐ Scheduling a quick values check-in with your team.
- ☐ Revising a policy to better reflect your CPoP.
- ☐ Recognizing someone for consistent, credible behavior.

Building consistency is not a one-time effort; it is a muscle. The more you exercise it, the stronger and more reliable it becomes. By intentionally reflecting and taking small actions, you transform consistency from a leadership buzzword into a lived, felt experience for every stakeholder.

Summary

Consistency is the third component in the EA Engine. It transforms where you are executing on your purpose and credibility from statements into repeatable, reliable action. You learned in this chapter how consistency builds trust, supports cultural alignment, and helps your values become tangible in every stakeholder interaction. Through Operational Credibility (aligning purpose, people, and processes) you can ensure that credibility lives not just in words, but in how your organization and you as a leader actually behave. By designing rituals, systems, and daily habits that reinforce what matters most, you create a trustworthy, resilient environment that can sustain abundance over time. Consistency is what makes your promise believable, again and again.

AHAs

- **AHA #13:** *Consistency is the silent engine of trust.*
- **AHA #14:** *Operational Credibility turns values into action.*
- **AHA #15:** When clarity and credibility meet consistency, your CPoP becomes unstoppable.

Chapter 6

Commitment: Sustaining Priorities Under Pressure

Introduction

If clarity defines where you are executing on your purpose, credibility builds belief in your ability to deliver on that purpose, and consistency makes it real day after day, then commitment is what sustains it all. Commitment is the fourth component in the EA Engine; the steady, unwavering force that keeps you moving forward, even when challenges arise.

Commitment is more than a declaration; it is purpose in action, demonstrated over time. It shows stakeholders (whether family and self, employees, customers, investors, and community) that you are not just here for a quick win, but for a long-term, meaningful mission. When people see that you stay true to your purpose despite shifting pressures or distractions, their trust and loyalty deepen.

In this chapter, you will explore how to turn the execution of your purpose into a sustained practice. You will learn how to embed commitment into the culture of your organization and your personal leadership habits, ensuring that Executive Abundance is not a one-time achievement but a lasting legacy.

Why Commitment Is Essential

Commitment is the difference between a flash of inspiration and a legacy of impact. Even with the best clarity, credibility, and consistency, execution of your purpose can stall without a long-term commitment to bring it to life … again and again. Stakeholders today are skeptical of initiatives that look good on paper but collapse under pressure. They want to see evidence that you and your organization will stand by your values, even when it is inconvenient, challenging, or costly.

Commitment signals resilience. It tells people that you are not chasing the next shiny trend, but that you are rooted in a meaningful mission. For employees, commitment creates a sense of security and belonging. For customers, it creates confidence that they can depend on you. For investors, it demonstrates discipline and a vision beyond quarterly results. And for your family and community, it models leadership with integrity.

Commitment Is the Fuel That Powers Purpose in Action

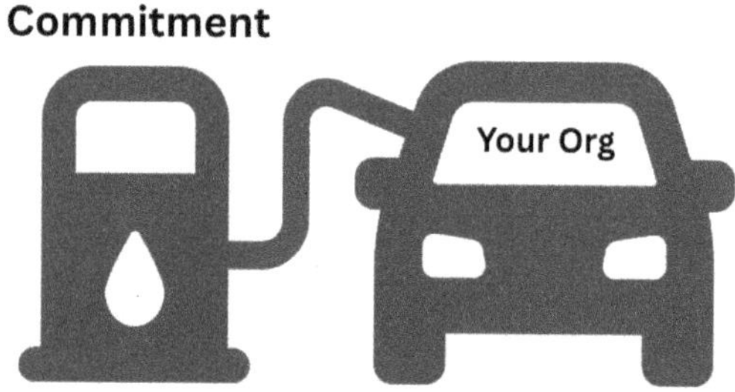

Figure 11: Commitment Is the Fuel

Short-term wins may feel rewarding, but true Executive Abundance requires a sustained, purpose-driven effort. Commitment is the promise that you will keep showing up, keep serving, and keep aligning your actions with your purpose no matter what.

Commitment is most visible when conditions tighten. When short-term pressure intensifies, the temptation to defer, dilute, or delay increases. Investments in people, culture, and long-horizon initiatives are often the first to be postponed in the name of immediacy. The retreat is rarely announced. It reveals itself over time.

Defining Purpose in Action

Commitment comes to life through purpose in action. It is not enough to articulate your purpose or even align your systems around it; you must live it. Purpose in action means turning that clarity and credibility into behaviors, choices, and practices that people can see and experience every day.

Purpose in action is how you demonstrate that your mission is real. It is visible in the decisions you make, the priorities you set, and how you treat people. For organizations, purpose in action shows up in hiring practices, customer service, partnerships, and how you invest in your community. For individuals, it shows up in how you lead meetings, support colleagues, and show up with authenticity and vulnerability.

When purpose becomes action, it becomes the most powerful credibility signal available. Stakeholders notice. They see that your mission is not a slogan but a lived reality. That is why purpose in action is the highest expression of commitment; it proves, over time, that you will deliver on your promises, no matter the obstacles.

Sustaining Momentum Over Time

Commitment is not a one-time burst of enthusiasm; it is an ongoing, disciplined practice sustained across cycles of scarcity and success. Even the clearest, most credible, and most consistent organizations can lose steam if they do not intentionally sustain their commitment over time, especially when performance pressure intensifies or results temporarily plateau.

One of the best ways to do this is through regular communication. Reaffirming your CPoP, celebrating milestones, and acknowledging challenges keeps the mission alive in people's minds. Quarterly CPoP reviews, leadership retreats, and town halls can serve as important touchpoints to remind everyone why you do what you do.

It is also crucial to adapt. Staying committed to your CPoP does not mean ignoring change; it means holding on to your core values while flexing tactics as the environment shifts. In times of performance pressure or market volatility, this discipline prevents short-term reactions from eroding long-term direction. Consistent commitment helps you navigate change without losing your identity.

Finally, celebrating progress is essential. Recognizing even small wins renews energy and reminds your team that their effort matters. Celebrations build hope, which is fuel for continued commitment.

When you make sustaining momentum a priority, you transform commitment from an aspiration into a habit and lay the groundwork for a legacy that lasts.

Building a Commitment Culture

Commitment is most powerful when it is shared. A truly purpose-driven organization or leader builds a culture where commitment is not just tops-down, but owned by everyone. This means empowering people to act on the mission, make values-based decisions, and feel personal responsibility for delivering on the organization's promises.

One way to build a commitment culture is to embed systems of accountability. When people know they will be held to purpose-aligned standards and that those standards apply to leaders as well, trust grows. Rituals like periodic values check-ins, peer coaching, and transparent performance reviews can reinforce this.

Storytelling is another powerful tool. Share stories of employees, teams, or customers who embody commitment. When people see real examples of purpose in action, they are inspired to live it themselves.

Above all, strong commitment cultures model resilience in the face of adversity. They do not abandon purpose during hard times, but rather double down on it as a guiding principle. That is how true Executive Abundance is sustained; through shared dedication, authentic ownership, and a relentless focus on serving all five stakeholder groups.

Reflection and Action

Commitment is not something you declare once and forget. It must be continually renewed and reinforced. Use these reflection questions to keep yourself and your organization anchored:

- Where have we let short-term pressures override our long-horizon commitments?
- What rituals or systems help us stay true to executing on our purpose, and where might we need to improve?
- How clearly do we communicate our commitment to stakeholders, especially during times of change or challenge?
- Are we consistently recognizing and celebrating people who demonstrate purpose in action?

Micro-Commitment:

Consider one micro-commitment you can make this week. Perhaps it's:

- [ ] Blocking time on your calendar to revisit your CPoP.

- ☐ Acknowledging someone who has modeled commitment.
- ☐ Holding a team conversation about sustaining their execution of purpose.

Commitment is a practice. By asking the hard questions and taking small, consistent steps, you transform where you are executing on your purpose from a statement into a living reality that people trust and believe in.

Summary

Commitment is the sustaining component of the EA Engine, transforming clarity, credibility, and consistency into a lasting legacy. In this chapter, you explored how commitment signals resilience, inspires trust, and proves that your execution of purpose is more than words … it is a practice lived over time. By defining purpose in action, reinforcing it through systems and rituals, and adapting while holding to core values, you create a culture that thrives through change and challenge. Commitment is what moves you beyond short-term wins toward building something meaningful, impactful, and enduring for every stakeholder you serve.

AHAs

- **AHA #16:** *Commitment is where your CPoP meets practice.*
- **AHA #17:** *Consistency without commitment is just routine.*
- **AHA #18:** *Purpose in action is the highest credibility signal you can give.*

Part 3

The EA Ecosystem: Family and Self, Employees, Customers, Investors, and Community

Part 2 defined how leadership should perform through the EA Engine: clarity, credibility, consistency, and commitment.

Part 3 turns to where that performance must hold.

Leadership is not expressed in isolation. It is tested across relationships. Every decision, communication, and trade off radiates outward into a system of interdependent stakeholders. This system is the EA Ecosystem: family and self, employees, customers, investors, and community.

Its order is intentional and interdependent. Strength at one level reinforces the next. Weakness at one level bleeds forward and backward.

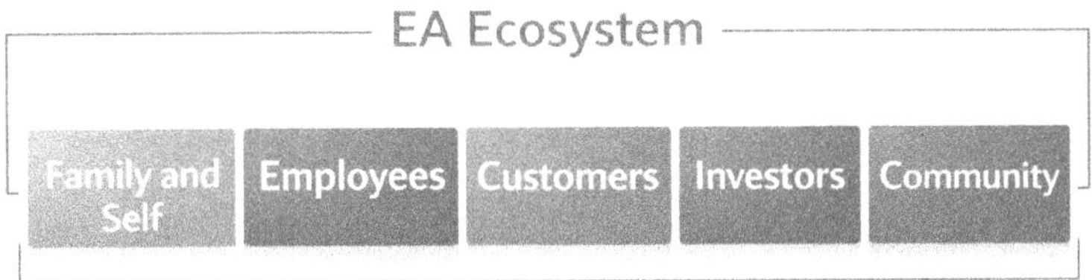

Figure 12. Ordered Interdependence Within the EA Ecosystem

When the EA Engine is intentionally applied across this ecosystem, alignment becomes durable. That interaction is the EA Framework.

This section shows you how leadership performance sustains coherence across all five stakeholder groups, beginning with yourself and extending outward to every relationship your decisions touch.

You will see how to lead yourself first, then empower employees to become partners in executing on that purpose. You will learn to serve customers with authentic, credible experiences, build investor relationships based on trust and long-horizon commitment, and extend your impact through community partnerships and networks.

This section weaves together everything you have learned so far and provides practical tools, reflection prompts, and AHAs to apply Executive Abundance across the full ecosystem.

Get ready to see how clarity, credibility, consistency, and commitment operate in the real world to transform leadership from a solitary pursuit into a pattern of service that strengthens every stakeholder it touches.

Chapter 7: Family and Self: The Internal Operating System of Leadership
Executive Abundance begins with the leader. Your health, clarity, and values alignment form your internal operating system. When that system is stable, leadership decisions flow with coherence. When it weakens, pressure eventually bleeds outward into every stakeholder relationship.

Chapter 8: Employees: The Organizational Operating System
Employees are the organizational operating system. When leaders reinforce clarity, credibility, consistency, and commitment internally, employees can execute with confidence. How they are treated shapes how the organization behaves under pressure and how purpose is translated into action.

Chapter 9: Customers: The External Test of Internal Alignment
Customers experience the culture employees create. When the internal and organizational operating systems are aligned, customers encounter purpose in action rather than positioning. Customer trust becomes the first visible signal of sustained coherence.

Chapter 10: Investors: Defending Long-Horizon Value Creation
Investors are fourth by design. When leaders strengthen the foundation beneath them, investor confidence becomes the outcome of system integrity rather than the starting point of decision making. Commitment protects that integrity when short-term pressure intensifies.

Chapter 11: Community: Extending Credibility Beyond the Enterprise
All of this unfolds within a broader physical and virtual community. Partnerships, referrals, and ecosystem relationships reveal whether leadership coherence travels beyond company walls or fragments under pressure.

The EA Ecosystem in Motion

The five stakeholder groups are not independent audiences. They are sequential and interdependent layers of reinforcement.

- It begins with you. Clarity stabilizes the leader.
- Employees experience that clarity first.
- Customers experience what employees internalize.
- Investors evaluate what customers sustain.
- Community reflects the cumulative integrity of the entire system.

The order is intentional.

Strength at one level reinforces the next. Weakness at one level bleeds forward and backward.

- When alignment holds across family and self, employees feel stability.
- When employees trust leadership, customers experience consistency.
- When customers trust the experience, investors see durable value.
- When investors align with long-horizon strategy, communities benefit from sustained contribution.

The EA Engine explains how leadership performs.

The EA Ecosystem reveals where that performance must hold.

Together, they form the EA Framework in action.

Coherence across stakeholders does not eliminate pressure. It prepares leadership to withstand it.

In this part, we explore how coherence across the EA Ecosystem becomes visible in practice, and how leadership patterns either reinforce or weaken that alignment over time.

Chapter 7

Family and Self: The Internal Operating System of Leadership

Introduction

Executive Abundance begins at home with you. Your family, your health, and your personal values form the foundation for how you show up as a leader. If you lack fulfillment or alignment within yourself, your leadership becomes brittle, reactive, and ultimately unsustainable. Executive Abundance starts by strengthening the integrated habits, beliefs, and disciplines that determine how you respond under pressure.

Your leadership begins with your internal operating system. Just as a company relies on an operating system to coordinate processes and maintain stability, leaders rely on their internal alignment to guide decisions under pressure. When that system is clear and coherent, performance flows. When that internal system fragments, pressure exposes the instability.

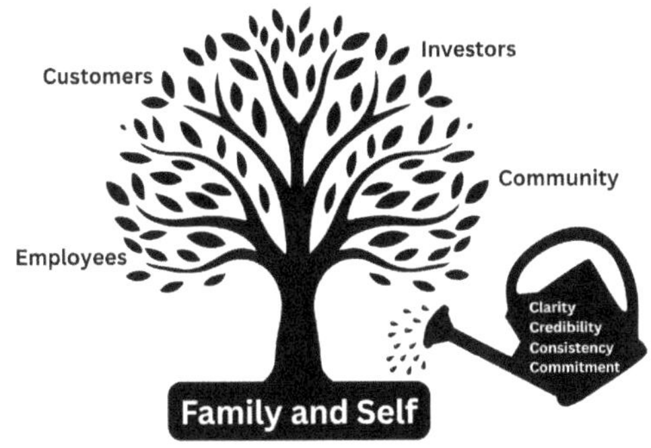

Figure 13: Your Internal Foundation of Abundance

Leaders often sacrifice their own well-being for external achievements, weakening the foundation from which they execute on their purpose. But what is gained if you burn out along the way, or leave your family behind? Investing in your personal purpose and nurturing your own reserves of resilience ensures that you have the energy to lead with consistency, credibility, and confidence.

This chapter will show you how to build and maintain habits, boundaries, and supportive relationships that protect your personal energy and align your purpose in action. When you invest in your own Executive Abundance, you model what authentic, sustainable leadership looks like and set the stage for every other stakeholder to thrive.

Building Personal Clarity

Personal clarity is the first step toward leading yourself with coherence, and by extension, leading others with authenticity and strength. Just as organizations must define where they are executing on their purpose through their CPoP, you as an individual need to articulate your personal CPoP. This means asking:

- Who do I serve in my life right now?
- What possibility am I creating for them and for myself?
- How does this possibility align with what truly fulfills me?

Your personal CPoP stabilizes your internal operating system when demands pull you in many directions. It offers a filter for decisions, priorities, and boundaries, reminding you of what matters most and what deserves your energy. When you define where you are executing on your purpose personally, you gain the confidence and clarity to show up powerfully in every other role you hold.

Without this clarity, it's easy to fall into overcommitment, chasing obligations that drain you or saying yes to things that do not serve your long-term mission. Leaders who fail to protect their personal clarity often find themselves slowly drifting, burned out, resentful, and disconnected from their deeper "why." Erosion rarely announces itself. It begins quietly, in small compromises and neglected boundaries.

- Investing the time to define your personal CPoP is not selfish, it is an act of responsible leadership. You cannot lead others toward personal abundance if you are lost in your own confusion or depleted by misaligned choices. Personal clarity is what makes where you execute on your purpose sustainable.

Living Personal Credibility

Living personal credibility means practicing what you preach, not only in your professional life but also in your personal relationships and private spaces. When your words and actions align consistently, you build trust with yourself, your family, and everyone around you.

At the personal level, credibility means your private behavior matches your public leadership. When your family experiences the same integrity your stakeholders see, your leadership gains depth and durability.

Authenticity is at the core of personal credibility. It requires the courage to show up as your true self, sharing your strengths and acknowledging your struggles. When you demonstrate honesty about who you are and what you stand for, your family and loved ones gain confidence in your leadership because they see you are real, not performing.

Integrity is equally vital. Credibility crumbles when there is a gap between what you promise and what you deliver, whether that is in a boardroom or at the dinner table. Being reliable, keeping commitments, and honoring your word shows those closest to you that they can depend on you.

Vulnerability and coachability are also key. It is powerful to admit you don't have all the answers and to be open to feedforward, even from family members. This models growth and creates a space where others feel safe to be authentic and to learn with you.

When you live personal credibility, you create alignment between your private self and your public self. This congruence makes it far easier to lead others, because you are not carrying the burden of maintaining a separate "leadership persona." You are simply being you, and that is what makes trust possible.

Sustaining Personal Consistency

Personal consistency is what transforms your clarity and credibility into a lived, dependable reality. It is not about perfection but about showing up in a steady, reliable way over time for yourself and for those you care about.

Consistency begins with habits. Daily rituals such as morning reflections, gratitude journaling, exercise, or regular family check-ins can anchor your connection to your purpose and remind you of what truly matters. These simple practices keep your energy focused and help prevent drift when life gets busy or stressful.

Boundaries are another foundation of personal consistency. Without clear limits, it is easy to get pulled off-purpose by demands that do not align with your values. Protect your time, protect your attention, and protect your energy so you can continue to lead from a place of strength and presence.

Finally, it is important to regularly check whether your actions match your personal CPoP. Take a moment each week to reflect:

- Did I live my CPoP this week?
- Where did I fall short, and why?
- How can I course-correct in the coming days?

Sustaining personal consistency is the discipline that protects pattern integrity in your leadership. When the people closest to you see that you live your values repeatedly, they believe in you and, more importantly, they believe in your mission.

Practicing Commitment to Family and Self

Commitment is the force that protects clarity, credibility, and consistency when pressure intensifies. When you practice commitment to yourself and your family, you build a foundation of trust and resilience that supports everything else you do.

Commitment starts with being intentional about where you spend your time and energy. Prioritize what truly matters (meaningful family connections, personal growth, and health) rather than letting busy schedules pull you away from executing on your purpose. Show up for the moments that matter, even when work is demanding or stress is high.

Purpose in action is just as important at home as it is in business. Your family, friends, and personal relationships are watching how you live your values. Demonstrate them through simple, powerful actions:

- Listen with presence and empathy.
- Keep promises and follow through.
- Apologize and repair when you fall short.
- Celebrate small wins and milestones together.

When you model commitment at home, you build a culture of personal abundance that extends into every area of your leadership. You show that purpose in action is not something you turn on and off but something you live everywhere, every day. This consistency strengthens trust and deepens bonds, giving you and those around you, the resilience to thrive.

Reflection and Action

Before moving forward, take time to reflect on how you are leading yourself today. Executive Abundance cannot exist without personal abundance. Use these questions as a mirror:

- Where do I feel most aligned with my personal CPoP?
- Where might I be overextended or disconnected from what matters?
- How am I demonstrating credibility at home through honesty, vulnerability, and follow-through?
- What consistent habits keep me grounded? Where might I build stronger routines?
- How am I showing commitment to my family and my own well-being?

Micro-Commitment:

Choose one micro-commitment this week to strengthen your personal foundation. It could be:

- ☐ Setting clearer boundaries.
- ☐ Scheduling intentional time with loved ones.
- ☐ Revisiting your personal CPoP.

Remember, how you lead yourself is how you lead others and investing in your own clarity, credibility, consistency, and commitment is the ultimate leadership act.

Summary

Executive Abundance starts from within. When your internal operating system is clear, credible, consistent, and committed, you create stability at the center. That stability does not stay personal. It radiates outward. In the next chapter, we move from the internal operating system of leadership to the organizational operating system, where employees experience firsthand whether your clarity, credibility, consistency, and commitment truly hold.

AHAs

- **AHA #19:** *Executive Abundance begins with personal abundance.*
- **AHA #20:** *You cannot pour from an empty cup. Lead yourself first.*
- **AHA #21:** *How you show up at home for your family and yourself shapes how you show up at work.*

Chapter 8

Employees: The Organizational Operating System

Introduction

Your employees are the beating heart of your organization's credibility. They are the first partners in translating your purpose from an idea into day-to-day actions and outcomes. If you fail to earn their trust and align their efforts with your mission, Executive Abundance will never gain traction beyond a PowerPoint slide.

Employees are the first external test of your internal stability. If your clarity is inconsistent or your credibility is performative, your team will feel it before anyone else.

Employees are hungry for a leadership approach that is authentic, transparent, and purpose-driven. They want to feel empowered to own their work, contribute ideas, and grow along with the organization. That empowerment can only happen when they see that your actions consistently match your words, and that you respect their voice in the larger mission.

This chapter will guide you through building credible cultures from the inside out. You'll explore practical ways to foster trust, encourage authentic dialogue, and align your employee experience with your CPoP (Customer Point of Possibilities). When employees are engaged and empowered, they become passionate stewards in executing your purpose, carrying Executive Abundance forward to every stakeholder they serve.

Building Clarity with Employees

Building clarity with employees begins with translating your own clarity into shared direction. Employees must not only hear where you are executing on your purpose, they must see how it guides real decisions. Clarity is the first and most essential gift you can offer your teams. When employees know exactly where the organization is executing on its purpose, through a clear and memorable CPoP, they can align their daily work with confidence and focus.

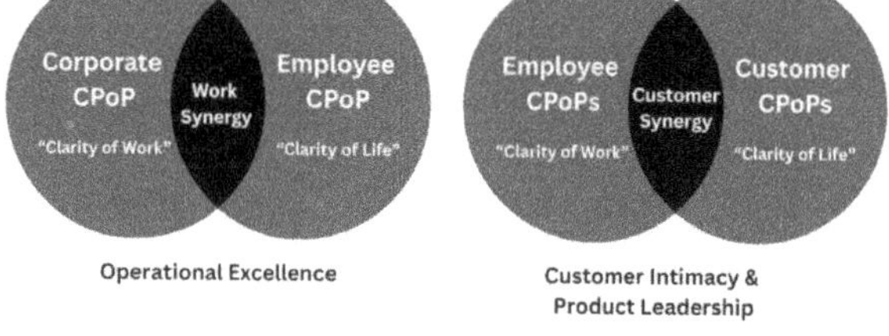

Figure 14: Employee & Customer Alignment

When leaders lack clarity, teams compensate with assumptions. Assumptions create fragmentation. Fragmentation erodes trust.

Start by communicating your organizational CPoP clearly, consistently, and repeatedly. Embed it in onboarding, performance conversations, team meetings, and recognition programs. When employees hear the same execution of purpose message in every setting, it becomes part of their thinking, their language, and their decision-making.

Employees watch patterns, not announcements. They track what gets rewarded, what gets tolerated, and what gets ignored.

Then, encourage employees to define their own personal CPoPs, a statement of who they serve and the possibility they unlock in their role. This personal clarity gives them a sense of ownership and helps them see how their contribution fits into the larger mission.

Finally, support this clarity with transparent communication. Share how strategic decisions connect to the CPoP. Explain why priorities shift, and how those shifts still honor executing on the purpose. When employees trust that leaders will tell them the truth, alignment becomes easier, faster, and stronger.

A culture of clarity transforms employees from passive participants to active partners in your mission. When they know where you are going and why, they will help you get there with energy, creativity, and heart.

Creating a Credible Culture

A credible culture is one where employees trust the organization and each other because integrity, fairness, and purpose in action are demonstrated repeatedly in decisions and daily behavior. It is built through daily choices, consistent behaviors, and leadership that models what it expects from others.

Leaders set the tone. If you want employees to live the 10 Credibility Values, you must live them first. Show up with authenticity. Admit mistakes. Keep your promises. Demonstrate that credibility is not a slogan, but a standard. When employees see this, they mirror it. Credibility is contagious.

Psychological safety is a cornerstone of a credible culture. People need to feel safe to share concerns, offer feedforward, and admit when they need help. This requires vulnerability from you and from your teams. When you encourage openness and protect those who speak up, you build trust that fuels innovation and collaboration.

Recognition is another powerful driver. Highlight and celebrate credible behaviors, not just financial performance. Recognize the employee who chose the "hard right" over the "easy wrong," or the team that supported each other through challenges. These stories reinforce the culture you want to build.

Finally, design systems that support credibility:

- Clear policies rooted in fairness.
- Transparent evaluations and promotions.
- Accessible avenues for feedback and improvement.

A credible culture does not happen by accident. It grows from deliberate actions, strong systems, and leadership that shows, day after day, what it means to put purpose in action.

Organizational erosion rarely begins with scandal. It begins when teams stop believing that today's priorities will still matter tomorrow.

Sustaining Consistency Across Teams

Consistency is what transforms a credible culture from a momentary achievement into durable pattern integrity. For employees, consistency creates confidence: they know what to expect, what is valued, and how to succeed. Without it, even a purpose-driven organization can feel unstable or unfair.

Start by designing simple rituals that reinforce your purpose and values. These might include:

- Weekly team huddles that link priorities back to the CPoP.
- Regular storytelling moments highlighting credible behaviors.
- Transparent updates on progress toward shared goals.

Consistency also lives in your feedback and feedforward loops. Encourage employees to voice when they see gaps between what the organization says and what it does. This helps catch small misalignments before they grow into credibility-killers.

Leaders play a key role in sustaining consistency. When they model the same values and expectations every day (not only during good times, but also under stress) they set a standard that others will follow. Consistency becomes part of the organization's DNA.

Finally, create accountability systems that support consistent behavior: fair processes, aligned incentives, and clear communication channels. These systems make it easier for employees to act with integrity and stay true to the organization's purpose in action, even as your business evolves.

Consistency across teams is the bridge between credibility and commitment; it ensures that employees experience the culture you promise, every single day.

Building Employee Commitment

Commitment is what protects alignment when short-term pressure tempts compromise. When employees feel invested, trusted, and empowered, they go beyond fulfilling tasks … they bring their hearts and minds to advance the organization's purpose in action.

Employees measure commitment not by enthusiasm, but by what leaders defend when tradeoffs appear.

Begin by empowering employees to execute on the organization's purpose. Give them the freedom to make decisions aligned with the organization's CPoP. When people feel trusted to use their judgment, they step up with greater ownership and creativity.

Share responsibility for outcomes. Invite employees to co-create solutions, involve them in setting goals, and make them part of the conversation on how to best serve stakeholders. Shared ownership builds shared commitment.

Invest in their growth. Help employees see a future for themselves within the execution of your purpose. Provide opportunities to learn, develop, and contribute in new ways. When people believe they can grow while making an impact, their commitment deepens.

Finally, celebrate their contributions. Recognize those who demonstrate commitment through purpose-aligned behavior. Small moments of appreciation, stories of impact, and meaningful acknowledgment reinforce that employees matter, their work matters, and their choices advance a bigger vision.

A culture of employee commitment is the visible expression of your clarity, credibility, consistency, and commitment in action. When employees believe in the mission and believe they have a role in achieving it, they become unstoppable allies in your journey toward Executive Abundance.

Reflection and Action

Creating a credible, purpose-driven employee culture requires more than intention, it demands continuous reflection and course correction. Use these questions to take a pulse check on your current environment:

- Where might we be sending mixed messages about our purpose in action or values?
- How clearly are employees connected to the organization's CPoP?
- What systems or rituals do we have in place to reinforce consistent, credible behavior?
- Do employees feel empowered to take ownership of our mission?

Micro-Commitment:

Choose one micro-commitment this week to strengthen employee culture. For example, you might:

- ☐ Open a discussion about values alignment during a team meeting.
- ☐ Revisit how you recognize purpose-driven behavior.
- ☐ Invite employees to define their own personal CPoPs.

The way you treat your employees (with clarity, credibility, consistency, and commitment) is how they will treat your customers, investors, and community. A credible culture starts on the inside, and it begins with you modeling the values you want to see.

Summary

Employees are a core stakeholder group within the EA Ecosystem. In this chapter, you explored how to empower them through clarity by aligning their roles and personal CPoPs with the organization's purpose. You saw how to build a credible culture rooted in trust, vulnerability, and consistent behavior, reinforced through fair systems and leadership modeling. You learned that sustaining consistency across teams creates confidence, while disciplined commitment transforms purpose from an idea into everyday practice.

When you invest in employees with intention and integrity, they become the stabilizing force that carries Executive Abundance across the broader Ecosystem. When employees experience coherence between what is said and what is done, they carry that coherence forward. Customers become the next ripple. In the following chapter, we examine how internal alignment becomes externally visible through the customer experience.

AHAs

- **AHA #22:** *Employees are a core stakeholder group within the Executive Abundance Ecosystem.*
- **AHA #23:** *Credibility is contagious; model it, and employees will live it.*
- **AHA #24:** *Culture is built one credible action at a time.*

Chapter 9

Customers: The External Test of Internal Alignment

Introduction

Customers are the external test of your internal alignment. They do not experience your strategy documents or leadership meetings. They experience your employees, your systems, your consistency, and your follow-through. If clarity and credibility hold internally, customers feel it immediately. If they do not, customers feel that too.

Customers do not encounter your intentions. They encounter your culture in action. What employees experience internally is what customers experience externally.

Too many organizations see customers only as sources of revenue, missing the opportunity to build meaningful, purpose-driven relationships that lead to loyalty and advocacy. When your employees are aligned and where your CPoP is clear, that intention shows up in every customer touchpoint, creating positive experiences that drive long-term growth.

In this chapter, you will explore how to embed your purpose in action and credibility into every customer interaction. From marketing messages to service delivery, you'll learn how to design consistent, authentic moments that build trust, reduce friction, and strengthen emotional connection. Customers who see your Executive Abundance in action become your most powerful advocates, helping to amplify your impact far beyond what you could achieve alone.

Building Clarity for Customers

Customers cannot trust what they do not understand. Clarity is the first and most powerful gift you can give them. When your customers know exactly what possibility you unlock for them (and why you are uniquely qualified to deliver it) they become more confident, more loyal, and more willing to engage.

Start by translating your organizational CPoP into language that resonates with customers. Instead of corporate jargon, speak directly to their pain points, hopes, and aspirations. Help them see the clear connection between their needs and where you are executing on your purpose.

Align all customer-facing functions (marketing, sales, service, and support) around this same clear message. Consistency of language and intention across every department prevents confusion and strengthens your brand. Customers should hear the same promise whether they talk to a salesperson, read your website, or interact with customer support.

Finally, set expectations transparently. Overpromising might win a short-term deal but damages credibility in the long run. Be honest about what you can deliver, the timeline, and the experience they can expect. When customers know what's coming and you deliver it, trust grows.

A clear, purpose-driven message helps customers feel valued, respected, and inspired. It sets the foundation for a relationship that goes far beyond transactions, grounded in shared possibility and mutual trust.

Delivering Credibility in Customer Experiences

Customer credibility is not built through messaging. It is built through lived experience, repeated interactions, and consistent delivery. It shows up every time a customer interacts with your brand; in the consistency of your service, the quality of your products, and the honesty of your communication. Customers want to know that what you promise matches what you deliver.

Train your teams to live the 10 Credibility Values in every customer interaction. Whether it is a frontline employee or a senior executive, everyone should demonstrate authenticity, integrity, respect, and a true commitment to helping the customer succeed. These values cannot be faked, customers sense real credibility instantly.

Be transparent, especially when mistakes happen. Customers do not expect perfection, but they do expect honesty. Owning up to problems, fixing them quickly, and communicating clearly builds far more loyalty than trying to cover them up. Vulnerability, when paired with a sincere effort to improve, strengthens relationships.

Use customer feedback as a credibility amplifier. Invite open, honest feedback through surveys, direct conversations, and reviews and then act on it. When customers see that their voices lead to real improvements, they trust you even more.

Ultimately, delivering credible experiences means customers feel respected and valued at every touchpoint. It is how you transform your brand from a name into a trusted partner, earning the kind of loyalty that fuels long-term abundance.

Sustaining Consistency Across Customer Journeys

Consistency is the hidden hero of exceptional customer relationships. It reassures customers that what they experienced once, they can count on again and again. Inconsistent service, on the other hand, breeds doubt and damages trust, no matter how good the occasional high point may be.

Design systems and processes that deliver predictable, high-integrity experiences every time. This means creating standards for how customers are welcomed, served, and supported. Document those standards, train for them, and reinforce them through recognition and accountability.

Watch out for "silo syndrome." When departments operate independently without sharing information, customers experience conflicting messages or uneven service quality. Break down those silos with cross-functional collaboration and shared purpose language rooted in your CPoP.

Build rituals for continuously improving the customer journey. For example, you might hold quarterly "customer experience retrospectives" where teams reflect on what worked, what fell short, and what can be refined.

Finally, measure consistency. Beyond satisfaction scores, consider tracking trust-based metrics like repeat purchases, customer referrals, or the quality of testimonials. These are powerful indicators of whether your consistency is building long-term confidence.

When you design for consistency, you do more than deliver transactions; you deliver trust, and that is what keeps customers coming back.

Customer erosion rarely begins with outrage. It begins with small disappointments that accumulate. A delayed response. An inconsistent promise. A moment where values appear optional. Over time, these small fractures weaken trust.

Building Customer Commitment

Customer commitment is earned when you defend alignment under pressure, not when conditions are easy. When customers believe in your CPoP and feel your genuine commitment to serving them, they respond in kind, becoming advocates and collaborators.

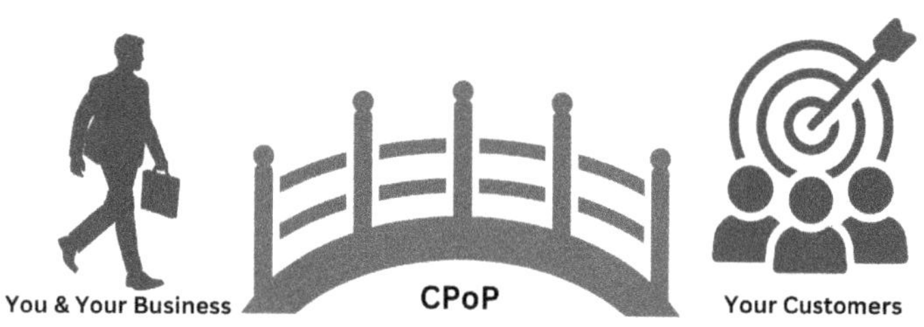

Figure 15: Collaboration Begins with Sharing Your CPoP

- **Invite customers into your mission.** Share your CPoP and show them how their success is directly tied to where you are executing on your purpose. Communicate not only what you do, but why you do it, and how their engagement contributes to something meaningful.
- **Encourage co-creation.** Give customers opportunities to provide input on products, services, or improvements. When people feel heard and see their ideas implemented, their sense of ownership deepens.
- **Share stories of impact.** Highlight how customers have achieved their goals through partnering with you. Celebrate their successes publicly, and let them share their own stories through testimonials, videos, or events. This builds authentic pride and belonging.

Finally, nurture relationships over time. Stay present, stay helpful, and stay invested ... even when there is no immediate sale on the table. Commitment means showing up consistently to support your customers, proving that their trust in you is well placed.

When you build this kind of commitment, you move from being a vendor to becoming a trusted partner, laying the foundation for Executive Abundance to extend beyond your walls.

Reflection and Action

Transforming customer relationships through Executive Abundance requires more than intention, it takes deliberate reflection and follow-through. Consider these questions as you assess your customer practices:

- Where might we be overpromising and underdelivering?
- How clear is our CPoP in the minds of our customers?
- Do our systems support consistency and trust across every touchpoint?
- Are we inviting customers to be true partners in our mission?

Micro-Commitment:

Choose one micro-commitment this week to strengthen customer relationships. It might be:

- ☐ Revisiting how you communicate expectations.
- ☐ Designing a feedback loop for continuous improvement.
- ☐ Celebrating a customer's success story.

Remember, your credibility and purpose come alive through every customer interaction. When you treat customers as partners (serving them with clarity, credibility, consistency, and commitment), you build the kind of trust that fuels long-term abundance for everyone involved.

Summary

Customers are more than buyers, they are partners in your mission. In this chapter, you explored how to build trust by serving customers with clarity, credibility, consistency, and commitment. You learned how to translate your CPoP into clear, relatable messaging, how to deliver experiences that align with your promises, and how to design systems that create reliable, trustworthy journeys. You also discovered ways to deepen customer commitment by celebrating their stories, inviting them into co-creation, and showing up consistently over time. When you treat customers as allies, you move beyond transactions to build authentic, purpose-driven partnerships that strengthen Executive Abundance.

When customers experience clarity, credibility, consistency, and commitment in action, trust compounds. Revenue becomes a byproduct of alignment rather than manipulation. Sustainable growth follows coherent leadership. In the next chapter, we examine how sustained customer trust strengthens investor confidence and supports long-horizon value creation.

AHAs

- **AHA #25:** *Customers remember consistent credible experiences, not empty promises.*
- **AHA #26:** *Trust is the foundation of every customer partnership.*
- **AHA #27:** *Consistency is the hidden hero of customer loyalty.*

Chapter 10

Investors: Defending Long-Horizon Value Creation

Introduction

Investors occupy the fourth position in the EA Ecosystem by design. By the time capital evaluates performance, leadership clarity, employee alignment, and customer trust should already be established. Investor confidence is strongest when it rests on that prior alignment rather than on short-term signals.

Short-term performance can attract capital. Long-horizon alignment sustains it. Investors who understand this distinction become partners in resilience rather than drivers of reactive behavior.

Too many boardrooms are still stuck in short-term thinking. The real challenge for leaders! Getting investors on board with a long-horizon, purpose-driven mission, and doing it without losing momentum or trust. By communicating clearly and consistently where you are executing on your purpose through your values and operational credibility, you help investors see the connection between stakeholder well-being and sustainable financial performance.

This chapter will guide you in reframing investor relationships beyond quarterly earnings. You'll discover strategies to build confidence through storytelling, reporting, and consistent behavior, showing investors that Executive Abundance is not a trade-off but a pathway to resilient, innovative growth. When investors trust your clarity, credibility, consistency, and commitment, they become allies in supporting your legacy.

Building Clarity for Investors

Investors need to clearly understand not only your financial vision but also why and how you intend to achieve it. A purpose-driven growth story creates confidence because it shows your strategy is rooted in more than opportunism; it is built on serving employees, customers, and the broader community.

Start by translating your CPoP into an investor narrative. Help them see how executing on your purpose guides decision-making and fuels sustainable results. Show that you have a reliable system for empowering employees and delivering consistent, credible customer experiences, which in turn supports predictable financial performance.

Be transparent about how you balance stakeholder needs. Investors appreciate clarity about trade-offs: for example, investing in employee well-being or customer loyalty may impact short-term margins but drive greater long-term value. Framing these choices through the lens of Executive Abundance helps investors see your commitment to responsible stewardship.

Clarity also means setting realistic expectations. Share what you will measure, what success looks like, and how you will adjust if challenges arise. When investors know what to expect and why, they trust that where you are executing on your purpose is not just marketing language, but a true guiding principle.

Demonstrating Credibility with Investors

Investor credibility is earned when transparency, performance, and stated values align consistently over time. Investors look for more than bold claims; they want evidence that you can execute on your purpose and deliver on your promises. That evidence comes from consistent, honest communication and transparent results.

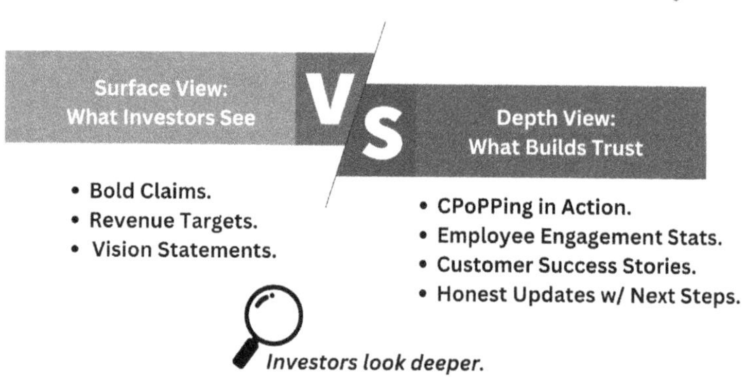

Figure 16: Trust Is Built on What You Do, Not Just What You Say

Investors study patterns. They observe how leadership responds when forecasts tighten, when markets fluctuate, and when tradeoffs surface.

Show your investors how your commitment to employees and customers supports financial performance. Highlight stories and data that demonstrate how credible leadership (rooted in your CPoP) drives retention, loyalty, innovation, and sustainable growth. When investors see the connection between stakeholder trust and predictable results, their confidence deepens.

Be honest about challenges and vulnerabilities. Investors appreciate leaders who tell the truth, especially when things don't go as planned. Share what went wrong, what you learned, and how you will improve. Vulnerability, when paired with a credible action plan, strengthens investor trust far more than spin ever could.

Finally, demonstrate integrity by keeping your word. Avoid overpromising in investor updates, make sure that how you execute on your purpose aligns with the numbers you deliver. When your narrative and performance match, investors see you as a leader they can trust ... not just for this quarter, but for the long haul.

Sustaining Consistency in Investor Relations

Consistency is the backbone of trust, especially in investor relationships. When investors see steady, purpose-aligned performance and messaging over time, they gain the confidence to commit their support beyond short-term results.

Short-term measurement systems can create narrowing pressure. If leadership begins managing optics rather than fundamentals, erosion begins quietly.

- Start by designing reliable reporting systems that go beyond financial data to include stakeholder indicators; employee engagement, customer trust, and community impact. These metrics prove that your purpose in action is being lived consistently, creating a more resilient business.

- Avoid "spin" in investor communications. Instead, adopt a discipline of transparent, values-aligned storytelling supported by data. If challenges arise, communicate them early and clearly, demonstrating how you plan to stay true to your CPoP while adapting to changing circumstances.

- Keep your messaging and actions consistent across cycles, resisting the temptation to chase hype or inflate numbers just to please investors. Consistency in executing on your purpose and delivering performance builds a foundation of trust that is stronger than any single quarterly result.

- Encourage a long-horizon mindset in your investor community. Share stories and evidence of how taking care of employees and customers fuels sustainable growth, reinforcing why Executive Abundance is a winning strategy over time.

When consistency becomes part of your investor relationships, you transform them from transactional funding sources to strategic partners invested in your purpose-driven future.

Building Investor Commitment

Investor commitment deepens when leadership defends long-horizon alignment, even when short-term pressure intensifies. When investors share your belief in purpose-driven growth, they become allies who champion your mission and support you through ups and downs.

Commitment protects consistency under capital scrutiny. It signals that purpose remains intact when quarterly tension rises.

Begin by inviting investors into your purpose story. Show them how your CPoP is realized through your employees and customers, and how this approach builds resilient, authentic value. Help them see that investing in your company is investing in a broader, meaningful mission that serves all stakeholders.

Demonstrate stewardship of their capital by transparently reporting how resources are used to reinforce the execution of your purpose. Investors are far more loyal when they see that their investment fuels a system of trust, innovation, and stakeholder success; not just short-term gains.

Share stories of how employees and customers thrive because of your culture, systems, and values. These stories give life to your numbers, making your impact tangible and relatable. It is easier for investors to stay committed when they see real evidence of how Executive Abundance translates into results.

Finally, seek out investors who align with your mission and are willing to co-create the future with you. Purpose-driven investors are more patient, more trusting, and more supportive of the long-term perspective Executive Abundance requires.

Sustainable returns are not the product of extraction. They are the product of coherence across the EA Ecosystem. When strength at one stakeholder level reinforces the next, capital becomes patient rather than impatient.

When you build this kind of investor commitment, you move from a purely financial transaction to a shared vision for meaningful, sustainable growth.

Reflection and Action

Investor relationships grounded in Executive Abundance require you to think beyond quarterly reports. Use these questions to reflect on your current investor practices:

- Are we making investor trust dependent on how we serve our employees and customers?
- Do we communicate where we are executing on our purpose and how it translates into performance, clearly and consistently?
- Where might we be sending mixed messages between our values and our financial reporting?
- How are we encouraging a long-term, purpose-driven mindset in our investors?

Micro-Commitment:

Identify one micro-commitment this week to strengthen these relationships. For example, you might:

- ☐ Share a story in your next investor update about how employees or customers benefited from executing on your purpose.
- ☐ Highlight stakeholder trust metrics alongside traditional financial data.

Remember, investors will trust you more when they see that you trust and invest in your people and your customers first. That is how Executive Abundance scales from a philosophy to a proven growth engine.

Summary

Investors are not just funding partners, they are participants in executing on your purpose. In this chapter, you explored how taking care of your employees, who then take care of your customers, creates the natural conditions for investor trust and long-term commitment. You learned how to communicate your CPoP as a clear, purpose-driven growth story, and how to demonstrate credibility through transparent, honest reporting. You saw that consistency (in messaging, performance, and values) builds confidence over time, while inviting investors to share in your mission transforms them from mere funders to true partners. When you lead with Executive Abundance, investors see sustainable growth built on a foundation of authentic stakeholder alignment.

When investors trust the integrity of your long-horizon strategy, capital becomes a stabilizing force rather than a destabilizing one. Yet no enterprise operates in isolation. In the next chapter, we extend Executive Abundance beyond capital markets and examine how credibility compounds within the broader community.

AHAs

- **AHA #28:** *Investors follow leaders who invest in people first.*
- **AHA #29:** *Trust flows from employees to customers to investors.*
- **AHA #30:** *Authenticity and stakeholder alignment build sustainable growth.*

Chapter 11

Community:
Extending Credibility Beyond the Enterprise

Introduction

Community occupies the fifth position in the EA Ecosystem. It reflects the cumulative integrity of leadership, employees, customers, and investors. When alignment holds across the first four stakeholder groups, credibility extends naturally beyond the enterprise walls.

Community trust is not built through announcements. It is built when stakeholders outside the organization experience consistency between what you claim and how you operate.

Too often, leaders overlook their community in favor of internal results or shareholder metrics. Yet a strong, trusted community acts as a stabilizing force, a source of authentic advocates, and a foundation for resilience during times of change. When you invest in building genuine relationships and supporting shared growth, you amplify your purpose in action exponentially. As someone recognized as the #1 Ecosystem Thought Leader by Thinkers360, I've seen firsthand how nurturing an ecosystem mindset within communities builds networks of support that are far stronger than any individual effort.

In this chapter, you'll explore how to extend your Executive Abundance outward into communities by aligning service, partnerships, and ecosystems around a unifying purpose. You'll see how legacy is not only measured by balance sheets, but by the positive ripple effects you leave behind ... impacts that outlive your leadership and strengthen everyone you touch.

Building Clarity for Community Engagement

Community engagement starts with radical clarity. Communities (whether local neighborhoods, industry alliances, or virtual networks) want to know exactly what you stand for and how you can serve them. If your message is vague, transactional, or unclear, trust will be slow to build, and impact will be limited.

Translate your organizational CPoP into a clear community narrative. Ask:

- How does our CPoP create possibility for the communities we touch?
- What specific issues or aspirations do these communities hold, and how does our CPoP align?
- What shared goals can we pursue together?

Identify where your CPoP and community needs overlap. For example, if you focus on empowering leaders, how can you help develop local leadership programs or virtual mentorship networks? If your CPoP is about credibility, how can you share those values with industry associations or online groups hungry for trust and authenticity?

Communicate this community CPoP openly and repeatedly. Communities, like customers and employees, need to hear the story often and in many forms to fully embrace it. Reinforce it through public statements, partnerships, and collaborative initiatives, so people see your CPoP is more than a marketing line; it is a living, breathing commitment.

This clarity lays the groundwork for deeper relationships, co-creation, and a shared sense of mission that strengthens Executive Abundance far beyond your own organization.

Demonstrating Credibility in Community Relationships

Community credibility is earned when your organizational behavior aligns with the broader expectations of fairness, responsibility, and contribution. Communities look for organizations and leaders who show up authentically, follow through on commitments, and act in alignment with their purpose.

Communities observe patterns over time. They notice whether prosperity is shared, whether commitments are honored, and whether impact is sustained beyond press releases.

- **Be transparent from the start.** Share what you hope to contribute, what you hope to learn, and how you will measure success together. Avoid transactional partnerships that focus only on publicity or quick wins. Instead, look for opportunities to build trust through shared goals and honest collaboration.
- **Show vulnerability by owning past missteps and demonstrating a commitment to improve.** Community partners respect leaders who are willing to learn and grow rather than pretend to have everything figured out.

- **Use storytelling to highlight credible behavior in action.** Share examples of how your CPoP has positively impacted community members, employees, or customers. Celebrate partners who embody your values, amplifying their stories as well as your own.
- **Build community relationships on shared purpose, not charity optics.** Communities can sense when a partnership is simply a PR move. True credibility is earned by being consistent, accountable, and genuinely invested in the people you serve.

When you lead with credibility, communities open their doors, invite you into authentic collaboration, and help expand your legacy far beyond what you could achieve alone.

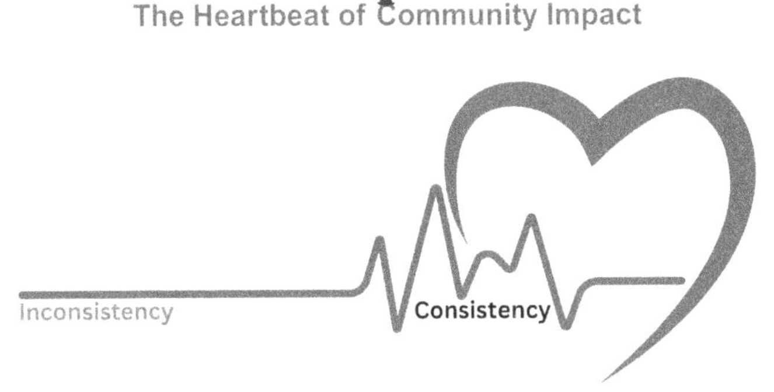

Figure 17: The Heartbeat of Community Impact

Sustaining Consistency in Community Impact

Consistency is what transforms community engagement from a one-time gesture into a trusted, long-term partnership. Communities (whether local or virtual) will only believe in your commitment if they see you show up, again and again, with integrity and follow-through. Community erosion rarely begins with public backlash. It begins when actions drift from stated commitments and small inconsistencies accumulate.

Avoid "one-off" projects designed only for publicity. Instead, embed community impact into your organizational culture. This means allocating resources, time, and leadership attention to community initiatives just as seriously as you do to customer or employee priorities.

Establish routines and rituals that reinforce your community commitments. For example:

- Schedule annual reviews of your community partnerships, asking what worked and what can be improved.
- Host quarterly roundtables with community representatives to gather feedback.
- Publicly share progress reports on your impact efforts, demonstrating transparency.

Measure community trust just as rigorously as you measure financial or operational performance. Are partners willing to refer you? Do community members speak positively about you? These signals are vital credibility indicators.

When you stay consistent (showing up with the same values, the same clarity, and the same integrity every time), your community relationships will deepen. That consistency becomes the bridge between intent and impact, proving that your Executive Abundance truly benefits everyone you touch.

Building Community Commitment

Community commitment is demonstrated when leadership defends long-horizon contribution, even when short-term pressures suggest withdrawal. When you invite community voices into decision-making and treat their goals as equally important, you build lasting, purpose-aligned relationships.

Commitment at this level signals that your CPoP extends beyond profit and persists across cycles of scarcity and success.

- **Start by involving community members and partners in shaping programs and initiatives.** Ask for their insights, listen deeply, and incorporate their perspectives into your planning. People support what they help create.
- **Demonstrate that your success benefits them, too.** Show how your growth provides opportunities; whether through jobs, education, collaboration, or positive influence. When communities see their aspirations reflected in your mission, they will invest their trust, time, and advocacy.
- **Respect is key.** Treat every community interaction with the same authenticity and consistency you would give a valued customer or employee. Avoid top-down approaches; instead, build relationships rooted in shared value and mutual respect.

- **Celebrate contributions from community partners.** Highlight their wins, elevate their stories, and shine a spotlight on the impact you've created together. This reinforces that your partnership is real, meaningful, and enduring.

By building commitment at the community level, you strengthen the EA Ecosystem and extend Executive Abundance beyond your organization.

Reflection and Action

Community impact is not about what you say, it is about what you repeatedly do. To build authentic, purpose-driven relationships with your physical and virtual communities, ask yourself:

- Are we building genuine partnerships or just making donations?
- How do our community initiatives align with our CPoP and our deeper purpose?
- Are we actively listening to community voices and incorporating their feedback?
- Where can we embed our community commitments more deeply into daily operations?

Micro-Commitment:

Choose one micro-commitment this week to strengthen community ties. It might be:

- ☐ Reaching out to a trusted partner for their perspective.
- ☐ Highlighting a community success story.
- ☐ Scheduling a quarterly review of your impact initiatives.

Remember, your Executive Abundance becomes truly powerful when it extends beyond your walls. Community relationships (grounded in clarity, credibility, consistency, and commitment) transform your purpose in action into a legacy that lives on for years to come.

Summary

Community impact is the visible culmination of clarity, credibility, consistency, and commitment expressed across the EA Ecosystem. In this chapter, you explored how to engage these communities with clarity, showing them where your purpose creates shared possibilities. You learned how to demonstrate credibility through authentic, transparent partnerships, and how consistency (showing up repeatedly with integrity) builds deep trust. You also discovered that true commitment means inviting communities into co-creation, honoring their voices, and demonstrating that your growth benefits them as well. When you treat communities as genuine partners, your purpose resonates far beyond your organization, becoming a powerful and lasting legacy.

When alignment holds across all five stakeholder groups, leadership achieves coherence. Yet coherence is most visible not in calm conditions, but under pressure. In Part 4, we examine how Executive Abundance either strengthens or fractures when external forces intensify.

AHAs

- **AHA #31:** *Communities amplify your purpose in action beyond profit.*
- **AHA #32:** *Referral partners accelerate trust faster than any cold campaign.*
- **AHA #33:** *Credibility compounds when you serve society as well as business.*

Part 4

Executive Abundance Under Pressure: Coherence in Practice

This Part is different from the others. Ten Executive Abundance case studies are bundled into a single chapter. Chapter 12 contains all ten.

Executive Abundance becomes clearest when leadership is tested.

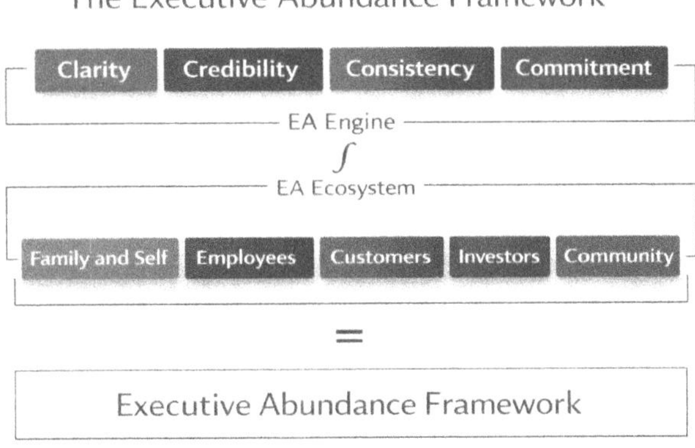

Figure 18. The Executive Abundance Framework

The case studies that follow examine how clarity, credibility, consistency, and commitment operate together under real-world conditions. Leadership alignment is not theoretical. It becomes visible through decisions, behaviors, and patterns sustained over time.

In Part 3, we explored the five stakeholder groups of the EA ecosystem in sequence. In this Part, coherence across those stakeholder groups becomes visible through lived leadership.

The cases are organized around clarity, credibility, and purpose in action because those elements are most visible externally. Within purpose in action, consistency and commitment become visible. What leaders repeat, defend, and protect determines whether alignment holds.

As you read, notice not only what strengthened alignment, but where subtle erosion might have begun if leaders had allowed incentives to narrow their focus or standards to drift.

Erosion rarely announces itself. It often begins quietly. Long-term investments become "revisitable next quarter." Language shifts from purpose to optics. Leaders defend metrics more than meaning. Development and well-being become discretionary. Inconsistency between message and action appears in small moments.

These are compression signals. The leaders in the following case studies did not eliminate pressure. They resisted narrowing under it.

Executive Abundance under pressure is not about perfection. It is about maintaining coherence when incentives narrow the horizon. It is about disciplined alignment sustained across cycles of scarcity and success. The question now is not whether this is possible, but whether you are prepared to lead this way when your moment of pressure arrives.

Case Study #1: Jeff Bezos at Amazon

When Jeff Bezos founded Amazon in 1994, the company's initial focus was selling books online. However, what followed was an unprecedented expansion into a global e-commerce and technology behemoth. Bezos's leadership, driven by a relentless focus on the customer and long-term thinking, created a new paradigm for corporate growth and innovation that embodied Executive Abundance.

CPoP: Customers Experiencing the Most Customer-Centric Company.

Case Study #2: Hubert Joly at Best Buy

When Hubert Joly became CEO of Best Buy in 2012, the company faced rapidly declining sales, growing online competition, and a disengaged internal culture. What followed was one of the most admired corporate turnarounds of the last decade, powered not by cost-cutting alone, but by a human-first approach that embodied Executive Abundance.

CPoP: Customers Seeking Technology that Improves Everyday Life.

Case Study #3: Hamdi Ulukaya at Chobani

When Hamdi Ulukaya, a Turkish-born immigrant entrepreneur, founded Chobani in 2005, he wasn't aiming to disrupt the food industry ... he was simply trying to bring better food to more people.

CPoP: Everyday People Deserving Better Food.

Case Study #4: Craig Jelinek at Costco

During his tenure as President and CEO from 2012 to 2024, Craig Jelinek quietly led one of the most respected companies in the retail industry. While other brands chased trends or quarterly headlines, Costco thrived by sticking to its values. Under Jelinek's leadership, the company scaled with integrity, delivering value not just to shareholders, but to every stakeholder group. His approach offers a textbook case of Executive Abundance in action; purpose-driven leadership built on clarity, credibility, consistency, and commitment.
CPoP: Value-Conscious Consumers Accessing Trusted Products at Fair Prices.

Case Study #5: Alan Mulally at Ford

When Alan Mulally stepped in as CEO of Ford Motor Company in 2006, the iconic automaker was facing what many considered an existential crisis. The company was bleeding billions, morale was low, silos were entrenched, and a global recession loomed. Yet, under Mulally's leadership, Ford not only survived ... it thrived. His approach exemplifies Executive Abundance in action.
CPoP: Customers Seeking Safe, Innovative, and Dependable Vehicles.

Case Study #6: Satya Nadella at Microsoft

When Satya Nadella became CEO of Microsoft in 2014, he stepped into a company with vast resources, iconic products, and global reach ... but also one facing cultural stagnation, internal silos, and a growing sense of irrelevance. Under his leadership, Microsoft didn't just rebound, it redefined itself. Nadella's approach exemplifies Executive Abundance in action, blending purpose, empathy, and consistent execution to realign Microsoft around its people, values, and mission.
CPoP: Every Org's Employees Empowered to Achieve More.

Case Study #7: Rose Marcario at Patagonia

From 2008 to 2020, Rose Marcario led Patagonia through a period of rapid growth and deepened purpose, tripling revenue while making environmental activism the company's organizing principle. Her leadership exemplifies Executive Abundance, built on bold clarity, lived credibility, and service to all stakeholders.
CPoP: Conscious Consumers Protecting the Planet Through Action.

Case Study #8: Indra Nooyi at PepsiCo

As Chairperson and CEO of PepsiCo from 2006 to 2018, Indra Nooyi led a strategic and cultural transformation of one of the world's largest food and beverage companies. Her tenure was marked by courage, clarity, and a commitment to reshaping what leadership looks like and whom it serves. Through her signature initiative, Performance with Purpose, Nooyi demonstrated that Executive Abundance is not only possible at scale, but essential to lasting impact.
CPoP: Global Consumers Striving for Healthier, More Sustainable Choices.

Case Study #9: Paul Polman at Unilever

When Paul Polman took over as CEO of Unilever in 2009, he made a radical choice: stop focusing on quarterly earnings and start optimizing for long-term societal value. In doing so, he transformed Unilever from a traditionally structured multinational into a pioneering model of stakeholder capitalism. His leadership is a compelling demonstration of Executive Abundance; purposefully aligning profit with people, planet, and long-term prosperity.

CPoP: Customers Seeking Sustainable Living.

Case Study #10: Garry Ridge at WD-40 Company

As CEO of WD-40 Company from 1997 to 2022, Garry Ridge transformed a single-product business into a globally respected, purpose-driven culture engine. His leadership exemplifies Executive Abundance in practice; rooted in clarity, operational credibility, and a deep commitment to people over politics.

CPoP: Customers Wanting Positive Lasting Memories.

Chapter 12

Executive Abundance Under Pressure: 10 Cases of Sustained Coherence

Case Study #01: Jeff Bezos at Amazon

When Jeff Bezos founded Amazon in 1994, the company's initial focus was selling books online. However, what followed was an unprecedented expansion into a global e-commerce and technology behemoth. Bezos's leadership, driven by a relentless focus on the customer and long-term thinking, created a new paradigm for corporate growth and innovation that embodied Executive Abundance.

Clarity: Earth's Most Customer-Centric Company

Bezos didn't just want to sell products; he wanted to create a fundamentally new way of doing business. From the very beginning, he defined Amazon's mission as:

"To be Earth's most customer-centric company."

This wasn't a slogan, it was a foundational principle that guided every decision. It shifted the company's focus from competing with existing retailers to reinventing the entire customer experience. This clarity created a flywheel effect of lower prices, wider selection, and greater convenience, reinforcing a consistent customer experience that attracted more customers and, in turn, more sellers.

In essence, this was Amazon's CPoP-in-Action.

If we applied the CPoP formula (see Chapter 3 for the full definition) to Amazon's leadership under Bezos, it might sound like: "Customers Experiencing the Most Customer-Centric Company."

This clear and unwavering mission gave every employee a guiding star. Whether they were in the warehouse, developing new software, or in customer service, their ultimate purpose was to serve the customer. This made decisions easier and faster, as they could be evaluated against a single, shared purpose.

Credibility: Leading with Customer Obsession, Innovation, and Long-Term Vision

Bezos didn't build credibility through charisma alone; he built it through a fanatical commitment to his principles. He famously left an empty chair in meetings to represent the customer, ensuring their voice was always present. He was known for his long-term thinking, often willing to sacrifice short-term profits for future growth. He instilled a culture of "Day 1" thinking, emphasizing that Amazon should always act with the urgency and innovation of a startup, no matter its size.

He embedded credibility into Amazon by making it relentlessly customer-focused, data-driven, and forward-looking.

- **Being Trusted:** Bezos's public focus on the customer and long-term shareholder value built trust with both customers and investors. His willingness to make large, risky bets (like AWS) and stick with them, even during periods of skepticism, showed his conviction and integrity.
- **Being Known:** His annual shareholder letters, filled with transparent insights and a consistent vision, made him a well-known and respected voice in the business world. He was the public face of Amazon, and his principles were synonymous with the company's.
- **Being Liked:** While not a "heart-centered" leader in the same vein as Joly (see case study #02), Bezos earned deep respect and loyalty through his intellectual rigor and consistent, principled leadership. His focus on hiring and empowering "builders" created a culture of ownership and innovation that others wanted to be a part of.

Purpose in Action: Serving All Five Stakeholder Groups

Jeff Bezos's strategy delivered value across every stakeholder group, albeit with a unique, long-term focus:

- **Family and Self:** Bezos's leadership was often described as intense, but he also emphasized the importance of work-life harmony and personal growth, encouraging employees to be lifelong learners and to take ownership of their careers.
- **Employees:** While Amazon's culture has been a subject of debate, it provided unprecedented career opportunities for millions of employees. The company invested in training and development, created new job categories, and empowered employees to innovate on behalf of the customer.

- **Customers:** This was the core of Bezos's strategy. Amazon's obsessive focus on the customer led to innovations like Prime, one-click ordering, and same-day delivery, fundamentally changing how people shop and live.
- **Investors:** Despite years of prioritizing growth over profits, Amazon's stock performance was one of the most successful in history, delivering astronomical returns for long-term investors. Bezos's focus on cash flow and market leadership ultimately created immense shareholder value.
- **Community:** Amazon's expansion created countless jobs in communities worldwide. The company also launched initiatives like its Climate Pledge, committing to significant environmental goals, and invested in local communities through various programs.

Purpose in action at Amazon was not episodic. It was sustained through repeated decisions that prioritized long-term value over short-term optics.

What We Can Learn from Bezos

Jeff Bezos's legacy at Amazon is an example worth repeating in building a company around a singular, long-term vision. He didn't just create an e-commerce giant; he established a new standard for how to scale a business by obsessively focusing on the customer above all else. His legacy demonstrates that by building a culture of relentless innovation and a "Day 1" mentality, a leader can create a business model that is constantly evolving and capable of dominating multiple industries.

Bezos's legacy also teaches us about the strategic value of earning and maintaining credibility through consistent, data-driven action. By transparently articulating his long-term vision through annual shareholder letters and making bold bets on new ideas like AWS, he built a deep trust with investors that allowed for massive, sustained growth. His legacy proves that a leader's most lasting impact is built on principled decision-making and a consistent alignment between their actions and their purpose, creating a blueprint for enduring success that outlives their time at the helm.

Bezos's leadership also reveals how easily erosion could have begun. Under similar growth pressures, companies often narrow focus to quarterly optics or dilute their founding principles. By defending long-term thinking and reinforcing customer obsession through consistent action, Amazon prevented fragmentation as it scaled. The lesson is not growth alone, but disciplined alignment sustained under pressure.

Case Study #02: Hubert Joly at Best Buy

When Hubert Joly became CEO of Best Buy in 2012, the company faced rapidly declining sales, growing online competition, and a disengaged internal culture. What followed was one of the most admired corporate turnarounds of the last decade, powered not by cost-cutting alone, but by a human-first approach that embodied Executive Abundance.

Clarity: Enriching Lives Through Technology, a CPoP-in-Action

Rather than fight for relevance through pricing or promotions, Joly redefined Best Buy's mission: "To enrich lives through technology by addressing key human needs."

This wasn't a tagline; it was a realignment of purpose. It shifted the focus from transactions to transformation, empowering employees to serve people, not just sell products.

In essence, this was Best Buy's mission.

If we applied the CPoP formula (see Chapter 3 for the full definition) to Best Buy's transformation under Joly, it might sound like: "Customers Seeking Technology That Improves Everyday Life."

This clarity gave every stakeholder (from store employees to investors) a reason to believe in the company's future. Decisions became easier to make and harder to misinterpret because they were tied to a shared, people-centered purpose.

Credibility: Leading with Love, Transparency, and Operational Integrity

Joly didn't begin with strategy decks; he began with listening. He visited stores, asked questions, and restored trust through presence and empathy. He avoided layoffs during early restructuring and emphasized internal reinvention over external blame. That human-centered approach extended even to partnerships, as he turned Amazon (once a feared competitor) into a strategic ally.

He rebuilt credibility by making Best Buy more human, more transparent, and more values-driven.

- **Being Trusted:** Joly faced hard truths publicly, protected jobs during downturns, and grounded his leadership in ethical decision-making. Employees and investors trusted him to act with integrity.

- **Being Known:** His visible presence in stores and willingness to speak openly about his values made him a relatable and accessible leader.
- **Being Liked:** His heart-centered leadership style earned deep loyalty and goodwill. By lifting up people rather than process alone, Joly fostered a culture others wanted to be part of.

Purpose in Action: Serving All Five Stakeholder Groups

Hubert Joly's turnaround strategy delivered value across every stakeholder group in the Executive Abundance Framework:

1. **Family and Self:** Joly practiced and promoted self-awareness, often referencing his personal journey and grounding decisions in mindfulness and emotional intelligence.
2. **Employees:** Wages were raised, local leadership was empowered, and store teams became central to the company's strategy. Culture became a measured KPI, not a soft afterthought.
3. **Customers:** The experience shifted from sales-focused to solutions-oriented. Employees were trained to ask, "How can I help?" rather than "What can I sell?"
4. **Investors:** Despite early skepticism, Best Buy saw its stock price more than triple, alongside improved margins and strong customer loyalty metrics.
5. **Community:** Joly expanded environmental commitments and launched initiatives to train youth in tech literacy, extending the company's impact well beyond its stores.

Joly's purpose in action was sustained through repeated decisions that prioritized people and long-term renewal over short-term financial optics.

What We Can Learn from Joly

Hubert Joly's legacy at Best Buy is a powerful testament to the idea that a leader can transform a company's financial fortunes by prioritizing people. He didn't just save a struggling retailer; he redefined what a corporate turnaround could be, proving that a human-first approach is a viable and lasting business strategy. His legacy is one of "unleashing human magic" by building a culture of trust and purpose, which ultimately created a sustainable advantage that outlived his tenure.

Joly's legacy also teaches us that a leader's credibility is built through actions that align with their stated values, especially in moments of crisis. By avoiding layoffs and focusing on empathy, he earned the deep loyalty of employees who then became the engine of the company's renewal. This demonstrates that a leader's most enduring legacy isn't measured in quarterly profits, but in the culture of trust and respect they institutionalize… a culture that enables a business to thrive long after they've moved on.

Joly's turnaround also illustrates how erosion might have accelerated under pressure. In moments of financial strain, leaders often retreat to cost-cutting alone or abandon purpose in favor of urgency. Instead, he reinforced clarity, rebuilt credibility with employees, and defended long-term alignment. By sustaining purpose in action rather than narrowing focus, Best Buy avoided fragmentation during a period when many expected collapse.

Case Study #03: Hamdi Ulukaya at Chobani

When Hamdi Ulukaya, a Turkish-born immigrant entrepreneur, founded Chobani in 2005, he wasn't aiming to disrupt the food industry ... he was simply trying to bring better food to more people.

Over the next decade, Ulukaya built one of the fastest-growing food companies in the U.S. through a deeply human-centered approach that exemplifies Executive Abundance. His leadership reflects the powerful interplay of clarity, credibility, and purpose in action, and what's possible when business becomes a force for good.

Clarity: "Better Food for More People"

Ulukaya's leadership was driven by a clear and unwavering purpose: make high-quality, nutritious food accessible to all, not just the privileged few. His internal compass (often expressed as "better food for more people"), was embedded into every facet of Chobani's identity, from product innovation to pricing strategy.

If we applied the CPoP formula (see Chapter 3 for the full definition) to Chobani's rise under Ulukaya, it might sound like: "Everyday People Deserving Better Food."

That expression of purpose was not just a marketing angle, it was a filter for action. Ulukaya refused to compromise on ingredient quality and ensured his yogurt remained affordable and widely distributed. Clarity wasn't about slogans. It was about making sure every decision, big or small, aligned with the mission to serve.

Credibility: Built on Action, Not Applause

Ulukaya earned credibility by doing what others wouldn't and doing it consistently. In 2016, he gave 10% equity in the company to employees, a decision rooted not in optics but in belief: that those who build the company should share in its success.

He offered generous parental leave, invested in community resources, and hired hundreds of refugees, later founding the Tent Partnership for Refugees to expand that work globally. These weren't PR plays, they were purpose in action. Ulukaya showed up as his authentic self, from factory visits to international stages, reinforcing trust through transparency and compassion.

His credibility spanned all three pillars:

- **Being Trusted:** Followed through on bold promises, from employee ownership to social advocacy.
- **Being Known:** Widely recognized for leading with empathy, vulnerability, and grounded leadership.
- **Being Liked:** Built goodwill through generous action, human connection, and moral courage.

Purpose in Action: Serving All Five Stakeholder Groups

1. **Family and Self:** Ulukaya stayed grounded in his identity and values, often saying, "Business is about human connection." His immigrant journey shaped his leadership, keeping purpose personal and present.
2. **Employees:** Profit-sharing, upward mobility, and factory-first focus created a culture of dignity, pride, and shared success. Employees weren't just workers, they were owners and ambassadors.
3. **Customers:** Chobani became a household name by offering affordable, clean-label yogurt with mass accessibility, proving health and quality don't need to come at a premium.
4. **Investors:** Despite being privately held, Chobani's brand dominance and growth made it a model for sustainable capitalism. Long-term trust and consistency drove success.
5. **Community:** From refugee hiring to rural economic revitalization, Chobani embedded its mission into every community it touched, extending its impact far beyond shelves.

What We Can Learn from Ulukaya

Hamdi Ulukaya's legacy at Chobani is a powerful example of how a business can be a force for social good while achieving immense commercial success. He didn't just build a yogurt company; he built a movement around the idea that "better food for more people" is a moral imperative, proving that a clear, values-driven purpose can be the most effective strategy for market disruption and growth. His legacy demonstrates that a company can win over customers and command a market by aligning its mission with a higher purpose.

Ulukaya's legacy also teaches us that a leader's most enduring impact is built on generous, authentic action sustained over time. His decision to give employees a share in the company's ownership and his commitment to hiring refugees created a culture of shared prosperity that inspired deep loyalty and respect. In moments of rapid growth and public scrutiny, many companies retreat to brand protection or short-term margin protection. Ulukaya did the opposite. He reinforced purpose through consistent action, ensuring that scale did not dilute values. His example reminds us that alignment must be defended as an organization grows, or erosion begins quietly at the edges.

Case Study #04: Craig Jelinek at Costco

During his tenure as President and CEO from 2012 to 2024, Craig Jelinek quietly led one of the most respected companies in the retail industry. While other brands chased trends or quarterly headlines, Costco thrived by sticking to its values. Under Jelinek's leadership, the company scaled with integrity, delivering value not just to shareholders, but to every stakeholder group. His approach offers a textbook case of Executive Abundance in action; purpose-driven leadership built on clarity, credibility, consistency, and commitment.

Clarity: Delivering Value with Purpose, a CPoP-in-Action

Under Craig Jelinek's leadership, Costco maintained an unwavering commitment to a singular purpose: delivering high-quality goods at fair prices to its members. This clarity wasn't expressed through elaborate mission statements or rebranding efforts, it was embedded in the company's actions. From pricing strategies to product sourcing, every decision pointed back to the same core promise.

In essence, this was Costco's CPoP-in-Action; a simple, operational expression of purpose that guided everything from merchandising to culture.

If we applied the CPoP formula (see Chapter 3 for the full definition) to Costco's evolution under Jelinek, it might sound like: "Value-Conscious Consumers Accessing Trusted Products at Fair Prices."

This clarity made alignment effortless across the organization. Whether it was launching Kirkland Signature, refusing to inflate margins, or prioritizing member trust over short-term gains, Jelinek ensured that Costco's strategy always served its purpose, consistently and credibly.

Credibility: Leading Through Integrity, Fairness, and Trust

Jelinek's leadership style was quiet but deeply credible. He didn't court attention or lead with charisma; he led with consistency, values, and fairness. His actions aligned with Costco's purpose and created a culture where trust could flourish.

1. **Being Trusted:** Costco was known for its pricing transparency, ethical sourcing, and refusal to use manipulative upselling tactics. Customers knew what to expect and got it.

2. **Being Known:** Internally and externally, Jelinek was known for standing by his people. He protected jobs, raised wages, and fostered a company culture built on mutual respect and operational excellence.
3. **Being Liked:** Costco regularly ranked among the top employers in retail. Employees cited high wages, internal promotion, and a sense of belonging: outcomes that stemmed directly from leadership credibility.

This trust wasn't marketing; it was lived reality, from the warehouse floor to the boardroom.

Purpose in Action: Serving All Five Stakeholder Groups

Costco's leadership under Jelinek consistently delivered value across all five stakeholder groups, a hallmark of Executive Abundance:

- **Family and Self:** Jelinek modeled work-life balance and prioritized employee well-being. Costco's compensation and benefits were unmatched in retail.
- **Employees:** Clear advancement paths, fair treatment, and shared success resulted in high engagement and low turnover.
- **Customers:** With renewal rates consistently above 90%, Costco earned deep loyalty by offering quality, simplicity, and transparency.
- **Investors:** A long-term, purpose-aligned strategy delivered reliable returns and steady growth, without sacrificing values.
- **Community:** Through sustainability practices, ethical sourcing, and philanthropy, Costco strengthened its role as a responsible corporate citizen.

What We Can Learn from Jelinek

Craig Jelinek's legacy at Costco is a powerful testament to the value of consistent, purpose-driven leadership. He didn't just run a successful retail company; he proved that a leader can achieve massive scale and financial success by quietly and consistently sticking to their core values. His legacy shows that a commitment to fair prices, ethical sourcing, and delivering on a simple promise can build a deeply loyal customer base and a respected brand that endures for the long term.

Jelinek's legacy also teaches us that a leader's most enduring impact is built on a foundation of trust and fairness, especially with employees. By providing exceptional wages, benefits, and opportunities for growth, he cultivated a culture of respect that resulted in high morale and low turnover. This demonstrates that a leader can create a legacy that outlasts their tenure not with grand gestures, but by building a system of trust and integrity where every stakeholder is valued, ensuring the company's "soul" remains intact even as it grows.

Costco's model also reveals where erosion might have quietly begun. Under margin pressure, many retailers trim labor costs, expand assortment indiscriminately, or chase short-term gains to satisfy quarterly expectations. Jelinek did the opposite. By reinforcing discipline in pricing, wages, and product selection, he protected alignment rather than diluting it. The lesson is not simply operational efficiency, but the courage to defend long-term value when short-term pressure intensifies.

Case Study #05: Alan Mulally at Ford

When Alan Mulally stepped in as CEO of Ford Motor Company in 2006, the iconic automaker was facing what many considered an existential crisis. The company was bleeding billions, morale was low, silos were entrenched, and a global recession loomed. Yet, under Mulally's leadership, Ford not only survived ... it thrived. His approach exemplifies *Executive Abundance* in action.

Clarity: One Ford, One Purpose

When Alan Mulally took the reins, he didn't waste time with abstract mission statements or vague corporate jargon. Instead, he introduced a unifying rally cry: "One Ford." It was clear, memorable, and actionable, a way to refocus the entire company around a shared vision. In essence, it was a CPoP-in-action. It meant one team, one plan, one goal: to create and deliver great vehicles that people wanted and valued.

If we applied the CPoP formula (see Chapter 3 for the full definition) to Ford's transformation under Mulally, it might sound like: "Customers Seeking Safe, Innovative, and Dependable Vehicles."

That expression of purpose, refined through the CPoP lens, reinforces clarity across all levels ... from design and engineering to marketing and customer service.

By uniting the company under "One Ford," Mulally delivered a powerful, CPoP-in-Action statement that gave everyone a clear line of sight between their daily work and the broader mission, a foundational move in building Executive Abundance.

Credibility: The Business Plan Review (BPR) as a Trust Engine

At the heart of Mulally's cultural turnaround was the weekly Business Plan Review (BPR). Every Thursday, Ford's senior leaders gathered to report honestly (using a red-yellow-green system) on their commitments and progress. No blame. No politics. Just clarity, honesty, and a commitment to *do the right thing.*

This was credibility operationalized:

- **Being Trusted:** Leaders were encouraged to admit when they were off track.
- **Being Known:** Everyone in the room knew where each project stood and who was owning it.
- **Being Liked:** Mutual respect was a core principle. Mulally often began meetings with warmth and humor, creating psychological safety.

In Executive Abundance terms, this ritual embodied Consistent Credibility (Step 2 of the EA Clarity Roadmap) and turned Ford's leadership into a stakeholder-aligned team rooted in trust.

Purpose in Action: Serving All Five Stakeholder Groups

Mulally didn't focus solely on Wall Street or quarterly returns. His model of abundance leadership touched every core stakeholder:

- **Family and Self:** Mulally led by example; optimistic, grounded, and emotionally intelligent. He created space for psychological safety and personal accountability.
- **Employees:** With his mantra "no jokes at anyone else's expense," he reshaped Ford's culture into one of dignity, collaboration, and candor. Employees were finally encouraged to bring truth to the table.
- **Customers:** Ford realigned product strategy to build cars people actually wanted; including fuel-efficient models and improved quality, backed by market research and clarity of purpose.
- **Investors:** Mulally famously refused a government bailout during the 2008 crisis, signaling financial responsibility and long-term thinking. He secured private financing ahead of the downturn, giving Ford breathing room to execute its strategy.
- **Community:** Ford reestablished itself as a responsible, values-driven corporate citizen. Its survival, without public bailout funds, became a point of national pride.

What We Can Learn from Mulally

Alan Mulally's legacy at Ford is a powerful testament to the idea that a leader's most significant achievement can be a cultural transformation that unifies an entire organization. He didn't just save a company from financial ruin; he replaced a siloed, blame-filled culture with one of transparency, trust, and collaboration. His legacy is the "One Ford" mentality, which proved that a clear, singular purpose can align every employee and department, creating a powerful engine for a company's renewal and long-term success.

Mulally's legacy also teaches us that credibility is operationalized through consistent, principled action. His weekly Business BPR was not just a meeting; it was a ritual that systematically built psychological safety and accountability, encouraging honest communication without fear of blame. This demonstrates that a leader can create a lasting legacy not through grand pronouncements, but by implementing simple, repeatable processes that embed core values like transparency and mutual respect into the very fabric of the company's daily operations.

Ford's crisis also reveals how erosion might have accelerated. In moments of severe financial strain, leaders often suppress bad news, protect silos, or shift blame to preserve authority. Mulally did the opposite. By insisting on transparency and reinforcing shared accountability, he prevented fragmentation when trust was most fragile. The lesson is not simply turnaround leadership, but the discipline to defend alignment when pressure tempts concealment.

Case Study #06: Satya Nadella at Microsoft

When Satya Nadella became CEO of Microsoft in 2014, he stepped into a company with vast resources, iconic products, and global reach; but also one facing cultural stagnation, internal silos, and a growing sense of irrelevance. Under his leadership, Microsoft didn't just rebound ... it redefined itself. Nadella's approach exemplifies Executive Abundance in action, blending purpose, empathy, and consistent execution to realign Microsoft around its people, values, and mission.

Clarity: Empowering the World, a CPoP-in-Action

One of Nadella's first moves as CEO was to shift Microsoft's mission from a product-centered vision to a purpose-centered one: "To empower every person and every organization on the planet to achieve more." This wasn't a corporate slogan, it was a CPoP-in-action. It provided a unifying lens for decisions, innovation, and leadership across all levels of the company.

If we applied the CPoP formula (see Chapter 3 for the full definition) to Microsoft's transformation under Nadella, it might sound like: "Every Org's Employees Empowered to Achieve More."

By rooting strategy in a purpose this clear, Nadella gave Microsoft a renewed sense of identity and direction. The company stopped chasing relevance and started creating it.

Credibility: Human-Centered Leadership That Built Trust

Nadella led with a unique approach to credibility anchored in empathy, humility, and consistency. Rather than command from the top, he invited employees and leaders into a more human, collaborative culture. He frequently spoke about the influence of raising a child with disabilities; an experience that helped him understand the power of listening, vulnerability, and inclusive thinking.

Internally, he replaced Microsoft's rigid, competitive ethos with a growth mindset, shifting from a "know-it-all" to a "learn-it-all" culture. Employees were encouraged to ask questions, admit mistakes, and work across boundaries. Externally, Microsoft prioritized transparent partnerships, customer-centric innovation, and long-term accountability.

This was credibility operationalized:

1. **Being Trusted:** Nadella built psychological safety by modeling humility and encouraging openness.
2. **Being Known:** He created a culture where people could show up authentically and share their ideas.
3. **Being Liked:** His warmth, emotional intelligence, and clear values made him not just respected, but genuinely admired.

This cultural consistency turned Microsoft's leadership team into a trust engine and set a new standard for corporate credibility at scale.

Purpose in Action: Serving All Five Stakeholder Groups

Nadella's leadership didn't focus on short-term wins or one audience alone. His purpose-driven approach activated Executive Abundance across all five stakeholder groups:

- **Family and Self:** Nadella emphasized personal awareness and emotional intelligence as essential leadership skills, bringing his full self to work and encouraging others to do the same.
- **Employees:** He led a cultural transformation centered on inclusion, growth, and collaboration. Employee engagement and innovation surged as a result.
- **Customers:** Microsoft realigned its offerings to be more cloud-based, interoperable, and user-friendly, building tools that solved real problems with real empathy.
- **Investors:** Purpose and performance coexisted. Under Nadella's leadership, Microsoft's market cap tripled within his first five years, showing that clarity and credibility drive real value.
- **Community:** Microsoft expanded its commitments to sustainability, accessibility, and digital equity, becoming a more responsible and values-driven global citizen.

What We Can Learn from Nadella

Satya Nadella's legacy at Microsoft is a powerful example of how a leader can revitalize a stagnant company by prioritizing cultural transformation. He didn't just retool product lines; he replaced a rigid, competitive ethos with a "learn-it-all" growth mindset, proving that a leader's most impactful work is often internal. His legacy is the re-energized culture of empathy, psychological safety, and collaboration he built, which enabled Microsoft to rediscover its purpose and reclaim its position as a global leader.

Nadella's legacy also teaches us the strategic power of leading with humility and emotional intelligence. By openly sharing his personal journey and modeling vulnerability, he built deep trust and credibility with employees and partners. This shows that a leader can create a lasting legacy not through a top-down, command-and-control style, but by fostering an inclusive and human-centered culture where people are empowered to achieve more, not just as a company, but as individuals.

Microsoft's transformation also reveals where erosion might have emerged. During strategic reinvention, organizations often cling to legacy dominance, protect internal hierarchies, or dilute accountability to preserve comfort. Nadella chose cultural transparency and disciplined focus instead. By reinforcing mission clarity and embedding empathy into leadership practice, he prevented fragmentation during transition. The lesson is not innovation alone, but sustained cultural alignment under competitive pressure.

Case Study #07: Rose Marcario at Patagonia

From 2008 to 2020, Rose Marcario led Patagonia through a period of rapid growth and deepened purpose, tripling revenue while making environmental activism the company's organizing principle. Her leadership exemplifies Executive Abundance; built on bold clarity, lived credibility, and service to all stakeholders.

Clarity: "We're in Business to Save Our Home Planet"

Patagonia's internal clarity under Marcario was unmistakable. Its rallying cry, "We're in business to save our home planet" wasn't just a tagline. It was a CPoP-in-Action that defined the company's purpose, product strategy, and social commitments.

If we applied the CPoP formula (see Chapter 3 for the full definition) to Patagonia's direction under Marcario, it might sound like: "Conscious Consumers Protecting the Planet Through Action."

This clarity was more than branding. It shaped the company's supply chain, marketing, hiring, and customer engagement. It invited every stakeholder (employee, customer, investor, or partner) into a larger mission. And it positioned Patagonia as not just a company, but a movement.

Credibility: Aligning Words, Culture, and Action

Marcario operationalized credibility at every level of the business. Under her leadership, Patagonia became a certified B Corp, re-engineered its supply chain for environmental integrity, and committed 1% of sales to grassroots environmental groups. In 2018, the company gave away its $10 million federal tax refund to organizations fighting climate change, a headline-making act of purpose in action.

Her credibility reflected all three pillars:

- **Being Trusted:** Backed bold environmental statements with real investments, legal action, and consistent ethical practices.
- **Being Known:** Publicly and internally recognized for modeling values-based leadership and radical transparency.
- **Being Liked:** Cultivated deep respect by centering employee well-being and creating space for activism and purpose-aligned choices.

Purpose in Action: Serving All Five Stakeholder Groups

1. **Family and Self:** Marcario led with personal alignment, frequently discussing her journey from private equity to mission-led leadership, proving that transformation begins within.
2. **Employees:** She championed family-first policies including on-site childcare, flexible schedules, and paid activism days ... making Patagonia one of the most admired employers in retail.
3. **Customers:** Patagonia's "buy less, buy better" philosophy invited customers into a cause, not just a sale ... deepening loyalty through shared values.
4. **Investors:** Though privately held, the company flourished financially. Profit was not the driver, but a result of credible operations and long-term trust.
5. **Community:** Patagonia became a powerful civic actor; launching lawsuits to protect public lands, funding climate action, and empowering grassroots campaigns.

What We Can Learn from Marcario

Rose Marcario's legacy at Patagonia is a powerful case study in how a leader can build a thriving, profitable business by making a bold purpose its central organizing principle. She didn't just grow the company; she transformed it into a global movement with the rallying cry "We're in business to save our home planet." Her legacy demonstrates that a leader can achieve radical success by aligning a company's entire operation (from supply chain to marketing) around a clear, unwavering mission that resonates with both employees and customers.

Marcario's legacy also teaches us that credibility is earned through consistent, courageous action, not just words. By giving away a tax refund to environmental groups, becoming a B Corp, and championing employee activism, she proved that Patagonia's values were not just a marketing tactic. This shows that a leader's most enduring legacy is built on a foundation of integrity and a willingness to operationalize their values, creating a brand that is not just admired, but deeply trusted and respected.

Marcario's leadership also reveals where erosion might have quietly emerged. In competitive markets, mission-driven companies often temper advocacy to avoid backlash or protect short-term revenue. Instead, Patagonia reinforced its environmental commitments even when they invited scrutiny. By sustaining clarity and aligning action with stated values, Marcario prevented dilution of purpose as the company grew. The lesson is not activism alone, but disciplined alignment when market pressure tempts moderation.

Case Study #08: Indra Nooyi at PepsiCo

As Chairperson and CEO of PepsiCo from 2006 to 2018, Indra Nooyi led a strategic and cultural transformation of one of the world's largest food and beverage companies. Her tenure was marked by courage, clarity, and a commitment to reshaping what leadership looks like and whom it serves. Through her signature initiative, Performance with Purpose, Nooyi demonstrated that Executive Abundance is not only possible at scale, but essential to lasting impact.

Clarity: Performance with Purpose, a CPoP-in-Action

Nooyi's guiding vision was both bold and precise: drive long-term financial performance while delivering positive societal and environmental impact. Her Performance with Purpose framework became a cornerstone of PepsiCo's strategic direction; influencing decisions across product development, sustainability, talent, and brand positioning.

It wasn't just messaging, this was PepsiCo's CPoP-in-Action.

If we applied the CPoP formula (see Chapter 3 for the full definition) to PepsiCo's transformation under Nooyi, it might sound like: "Global Consumers Striving for Healthier, More Sustainable Choices."

This clarity showed up in the way PepsiCo reformulated products, acquired purpose-aligned brands like Quaker and Tropicana, and embedded sustainability into supply chains. With a clearly defined north star, Nooyi gave every stakeholder (from board members to frontline employees) a reason to believe in where the company was going and why it mattered.

Credibility: Strategic Risks Backed by Consistent Action

Nooyi's credibility was forged in trade-offs. In a market obsessed with short-term returns, she championed long-term investments in health, inclusion, and sustainability, even when critics doubted her.

Internally, she built a culture of care and accountability. She famously wrote more than 400 personal letters to the parents of her executive team, modeling humility, gratitude, and connection. She openly shared the complexities of balancing leadership with family life, giving permission for others to show up as whole, authentic people.

Nooyi didn't just talk about values, she operationalized them. And through repeated, consistent action, she built trust at every level of the organization.

1. **Being Trusted:** Nooyi stayed committed to long-term change even when Wall Street resisted. Her consistency and discipline signaled integrity across the board.
2. **Being Known:** She made herself relatable and visible, not just as a CEO, but as a human being. Her transparency and accessibility helped define the culture she wanted to lead.
3. **Being Liked:** Acts of personal care, like handwritten letters and inclusive policies, created deep connection and loyalty within the organization.

Purpose in Action: Serving All Five Stakeholder Groups

Indra Nooyi's leadership consistently delivered value to each of the five stakeholder groups foundational to Executive Abundance:

- **Family and Self:** Nooyi led with emotional intelligence, transparency, and a deep understanding of the pressures faced by modern leaders, particularly women and parents. Her openness inspired a more human approach to executive life.
- **Employees:** PepsiCo advanced DEI efforts, launched internal leadership programs, and prioritized employee wellness. Her people-first philosophy became embedded in hiring, retention, and development practices.
- **Customers:** From reduced sugar and sodium to eco-friendly packaging, PepsiCo evolved its offerings in direct response to changing consumer values, fulfilling the company's CPoP through innovation and transparency.
- **Investors:** Despite initial skepticism, Nooyi grew revenue by more than 80% during her tenure. She proved that performance and purpose are not competing goals, but complementary levers of lasting value.
- **Community:** Through initiatives focused on water conservation, women's empowerment, and global sustainability, PepsiCo deepened its impact beyond the business; reaching millions of lives worldwide.

What We Can Learn from Nooyi

Indra Nooyi's legacy at PepsiCo is a testament to the power of a leader's strategic vision to not only drive business success but also to reshape an entire industry's priorities. Through her "Performance with Purpose" initiative, she proved that a company can achieve robust financial growth while simultaneously making a positive social and environmental impact. Her legacy demonstrates that a leader can create a sustainable competitive advantage by clearly defining a purpose that addresses evolving consumer values and positions the company for long-term relevance.

Nooyi's legacy also teaches us the importance of leading with both courage and compassion. She was willing to make tough, long-term strategic decisions in the face of short-term criticism, and she operationalized her values through personal acts of care, like writing letters to her executives' families. This shows that a leader's most enduring legacy is built on a foundation of integrity and empathy, creating a culture of trust and authenticity that inspires employees and helps a company thrive long after the leader has moved on.

Nooyi's tenure also shows where erosion might have taken hold. Under activist pressure and quarterly scrutiny, leaders often delay transformation or soften long-term commitments to preserve near-term performance. Instead, she reinforced clarity around Performance with Purpose and sustained alignment through measurable action. By resisting short-term appeasement, she prevented strategic drift during a period when compromise would have been easier. The lesson is not ambition alone, but the discipline to protect long-horizon direction under investor pressure.

Case Study #09: Paul Polman at Unilever

When Paul Polman took over as CEO of Unilever in 2009, he made a radical choice: stop focusing on quarterly earnings and start optimizing for long-term societal value. In doing so, he transformed Unilever from a traditionally structured multinational into a pioneering model of stakeholder capitalism. His leadership is a compelling demonstration of Executive Abundance, purposefully aligning profit with people, planet, and long-term prosperity.

Clarity: A CPoP-in-Action, Sustainable Living as Strategy

Polman reframed Unilever's north star around a simple, compelling idea: "To make sustainable living commonplace."

This wasn't just a mission statement, it was clarity in action. It gave direction to every part of the business: product reformulation, packaging design, supply chain partnerships, employee incentives, and brand positioning.

If we applied the CPoP formula (see Chapter 3 for the full definition) to Unilever's transformation under Polman, it might sound like: "Customers Seeking Sustainable Living."

This CPoP, whether explicitly stated or not, functioned as the organizing principle behind Unilever's largest strategic bet: that doing good could drive market leadership and that clarity around who they served and why would unlock innovation, resilience, and relevance.

Credibility: Walking the Talk on ESG Before It Was Trendy

Polman operationalized his values through bold choices. He launched the Unilever Sustainable Living Plan, which committed the company to measurable goals, like halving its environmental footprint and improving the health and well-being of over a billion people. He changed leadership compensation models and resisted investor pressure to return to short-term metrics, prioritizing consistency over convenience.

- **Being Trusted:** Polman consistently chose long-term purpose over short-term gain, backing up his promises with transparent goals and measurable progress.
- **Being Known:** Through public advocacy and internal alignment, he made Unilever's values visible and accessible, both within the company and to the wider public.
- **Being Liked:** His moral clarity, humility, and emphasis on service made him widely respected by employees, NGOs, and peers. He led with both intellect and heart.

Purpose in Action: Serving All Five Stakeholder Groups

Polman's decisions consistently reflected the full Executive Abundance model, with positive impact across all five stakeholder groups:

1. **Family and Self:** Polman emphasized moral responsibility and modeled humility and authenticity as core traits of leadership.
2. **Employees:** Purpose was embedded into individual roles, with innovation and performance incentives aligned to sustainability outcomes. Employees felt part of something larger than profit.
3. **Customers:** Products were reformulated to meet growing consumer demand for ethical, sustainable brands, with transparency and wellness at the core.
4. **Investors:** Over time, Unilever's long-term orientation paid off, with strong returns and resilience. Polman showed that stakeholder capitalism could be a superior business model.
5. **Community:** The company led global partnerships addressing water access, hygiene, gender equity, and poverty ... proving that business can be a force for good.

What We Can Learn from Polman

Paul Polman's legacy at Unilever is a powerful testament to the idea that a leader can transform a company's success by redefining its purpose from profit to people and the planet. He didn't just manage a consumer goods giant; he launched a global movement by committing the company to "make sustainable living commonplace." His legacy demonstrates that a leader can build long-term value and market leadership by making a bold, purpose-driven mission the central organizing principle of a business.

Polman's legacy also teaches us that true credibility is built through courageous, consistent action that prioritizes long-term value over short-term gain. He famously resisted pressure for quarterly results and instead focused on measurable sustainability goals, proving that a leader can earn deep trust from all stakeholders by living their values, even when it's difficult. This shows that a leader's most enduring impact is not in their financial results, but in their ability to fundamentally change a company's purpose and culture to create a more resilient and responsible model for business.

Polman's tenure also reveals where erosion might have quietly begun. In public markets, leaders often revert to quarterly signaling when investor confidence wavers, narrowing ambition to reassure analysts. That subtle shift can fragment purpose from performance. Polman resisted that pressure. By defending long-horizon sustainability and aligning capital decisions with stated values, he prevented drift between rhetoric and reality. The lesson is not sustainability alone, but disciplined alignment when capital markets test resolve.

Case Study #10: Garry Ridge at WD-40 Company

As CEO of WD-40 Company from 1997 to 2022, Garry Ridge transformed a single-product business into a globally respected, purpose-driven culture engine. His leadership exemplifies Executive Abundance in practice; rooted in clarity, operational credibility, consistency, and a deep commitment to people over politics.

Clarity: "Creating Positive, Lasting Memories"

WD-40 Company's purpose under Ridge was bold, emotional, and actionable: "We exist to create positive lasting memories in everything we do." More than a mission statement, this became a decision-making lens across the company. It clarified how the organization served customers, collaborated internally, and contributed to the world.

If we applied the CPoP formula (see Chapter 3 for the full definition) to WD-40 Company's evolution under Ridge, it might sound like: "Customers Wanting Positive, Lasting Memories."

This CPoP-in-action was lived daily, whether through customer support calls or product innovation. It gave every employee a reason to feel proud, and it infused even mundane tasks with meaning.

Credibility: Trust as a Leadership Standard

Garry Ridge built a company culture rooted in the three pillars of credibility: being Trusted, Known, and Liked.

- **Being Trusted:** Ridge normalized vulnerability at the top. He openly shared mistakes and reframed them as "learning moments," creating psychological safety for others to do the same.
- **Being Known:** Feedback was encouraged, not punished. Every team member was expected to grow, contribute, and speak up.
- **Being Liked:** Respect and dignity weren't aspirational values; they were practiced daily. Ridge often referred to employees as part of a "tribe," reinforcing a sense of belonging and shared purpose.

His personal humility and emotional intelligence served as cultural anchors for the organization.

Purpose in Action: Serving All Five Stakeholder Groups

1. **Family and Self:** Ridge emphasized the importance of self-reflection, emotional intelligence, and the development of the "whole person." His leadership style encouraged self-awareness as a key lever for sustainable leadership.
2. **Employees:** WD-40 Company invested heavily in internal leadership development, coaching, and team cohesion. Engagement scores were consistently among the highest in the world.
3. **Customers:** The company didn't chase transactions, it focused on creating trust. Its legendary product reliability was matched by human-first customer service.
4. **Investors:** Under Ridge, WD-40 Company delivered consistent profitability and global expansion, with clarity and purpose driving performance, not quarterly pressure.
5. **Community:** Employees were encouraged to contribute to their communities, and Ridge himself invested in mentoring, thought leadership, and values-based impact beyond the company walls.

What We Can Learn from Ridge

Garry Ridge's legacy at WD-40 Company clearly demonstrates how a leader can transform a business by making culture its most valuable asset. He didn't just sell a product; he built a "tribe" around a deeply human purpose of "creating positive, lasting memories." His legacy demonstrates that a leader can achieve global success and long-term profitability by consistently prioritizing people over politics, proving that an emotionally intelligent, purpose-driven culture is the ultimate competitive advantage.

Ridge's legacy also teaches us that credibility is built on a foundation of psychological safety and shared purpose. By openly sharing his own mistakes and encouraging a culture of "learning moments," he created an environment where employees felt safe to contribute, innovate, and grow. This shows that a leader's most enduring impact is the culture of trust, respect, and belonging they leave behind, a culture that empowers every team member to become a leader themselves.

Ridge's leadership also highlights where erosion might have quietly emerged. In long-tenured success stories, complacency often replaces curiosity, and culture becomes slogan rather than practice. Comfort can dilute discipline. Ridge resisted that drift by reinforcing learning rituals and modeling vulnerability consistently over time. By sustaining alignment even in periods of stability, he prevented quiet cultural decay. The lesson is not longevity alone, but the discipline to renew culture before stagnation sets in.

Reflection and Action

Before moving forward, pause and reflect on the patterns across the ten leaders in this chapter. Each faced a different form of pressure such as scale, crisis, scrutiny, disruption, or cultural drift. In every case, alignment either strengthened under that pressure or could have fractured. The difference was not circumstance, but disciplined leadership sustained over time.

Use the questions below to reflect on how these stories intersect with your own leadership journey:

- Which leader's story resonated most with your current leadership challenges and why?
- If your company's CPoP were made visible through daily behavior, what would people see?
- Where are you showing credibility through action and where might trust be slipping?
- Are you serving all five stakeholder groups or over-indexing on just one?
- What's one system or ritual you could introduce (or revive) to embed purpose deeper into your organization?

Micro-Commitment

Pick one small step you can take this week to apply what you've learned from these case studies:

- ☐ Share one of these stories with your team and spark a discussion about purpose in action.
- ☐ Revisit your stakeholder strategy and identify where clarity or trust needs reinforcement.
- ☐ Ask your team: "What would Executive Abundance look like here?"
- ☐ Name and celebrate one example of credibility you've seen in action recently and why it matters.

Executive Abundance is not a leadership theory, it's a lived pattern. Let these case studies serve not just as inspiration, but as a call to practice: to lead with more intentionality, integrity, and clarity in every decision, conversation, and system you shape.

Summary

The ten leaders in this chapter demonstrate that Executive Abundance is not revealed in calm conditions. It becomes visible when pressure intensifies and tradeoffs sharpen. In those moments, clarity, credibility, consistency, and commitment either reinforce one another or begin to drift apart.

These case studies show the EA Engine and the EA Ecosystem in action. Across industries and contexts, strength at one stakeholder level reinforced the next. Alignment sustained under pressure created durable performance. Where alignment could have narrowed, disciplined leadership prevented quiet erosion.

Executive Abundance under pressure is not about perfection. It is about coherence sustained over time.

AHAs

- **AHA #34:** *Clarity is a force multiplier.*
- **AHA #35:** *Credibility is earned through consistent behavior.*
- **AHA #36:** *Purpose in action becomes real when it shows up in systems, not just speeches.*

Part 5

Sustaining Executive Abundance Across Cycles

You've built clarity, credibility, consistency, and commitment. You've seen how Executive Abundance strengthens stakeholder relationships and holds under pressure. The question now is not whether it works. The question is whether it endures.

Part 5 moves from understanding to sustainability.

You will learn how to embed alignment into your operating rhythm so it does not depend on personality or momentum. You will also see how to multiply Executive Abundance across your leadership system. And how disciplined reinforcement shapes legacy over time.

Executive Abundance must hold not only in moments of growth, but across cycles of scarcity, stability, and success.

Chapter 13: Sustaining Executive Abundance: Embedding Alignment Into Operating Rhythm
Chapter 13 focuses on institutionalizing clarity, credibility, consistency, and commitment so alignment remains strong even as circumstances change. You'll explore habits, accountability structures, and operating rhythms that protect coherence across stakeholders.

Chapter 14: Multiplying Executive Abundance Across the Leadership System
Chapter 14 expands Executive Abundance beyond the individual leader. You'll learn how to distribute ownership of the EA Engine, embed credibility values into systems, and ensure alignment strengthens across leadership layers and ecosystem partners.

Chapter 15: What You Reinforce Becomes Your Legacy
In Chapter 15, you'll examine how measurement, celebration, and reinforcement determine what endures. You'll discover how stakeholder success becomes the clearest expression of legacy, and how what you consistently reinforce shapes culture long after you leave the room.

Chapter 13

Sustaining Executive Abundance: Embedding Alignment Into Operating Rhythm

Introduction

Executive Abundance becomes sustainable when the EA Engine and the EA Ecosystem operate together in rhythm.

Clarity, credibility, consistency, and commitment define how leadership performs. Family and self, employees, customers, investors, and community define where that performance must hold. When these two dimensions reinforce one another, alignment becomes durable rather than situational.

In Part 4, you saw leaders sustain coherence in crisis, in rapid growth, and in long-term stability. Different pressures. Same architecture.

But many organizations depend on a single leader as the stabilizing force. The leader is the energy. The leader is the discipline. The leader is the culture carrier. And when that leader leaves, coherence weakens and patterns fragment.

Executive Abundance cannot depend on personality.

This chapter focuses on embedding alignment into your operating rhythm so it does not depend on personality, mood, or circumstance. It must be systemic.

- Cycles of scarcity test your integrity.
- Cycles of success test your focus.
- Periods of stability test your vigilance.

Erosion rarely begins dramatically. It begins subtly. A standard slips. A stakeholder is deprioritized. A system becomes optional. Left unattended, that weakness spreads forward and backward through the ecosystem.

Here, we move from inspiration to implementation. We focus on building systems, habits, and reinforcement patterns that allow the EA Engine to hold across the EA Ecosystem, cycle after cycle, across leadership transitions.

Refreshing Your CPoP Over Time

Your CPoP (Customer Point of Possibilities) is the beating heart of Executive Abundance. But even the strongest execution of your purpose statements can grow stale if they aren't revisited and refreshed over time. Markets change, customer expectations evolve, and your stakeholders shift. Your CPoP must adapt to stay relevant and inspiring.

Refreshing your CPoP is not about chasing trends or rebranding for attention. It is about ensuring that clarity continues to align the EA Engine across the EA Ecosystem. When clarity drifts from stakeholder reality, the ecosystem fragments. When clarity remains anchored to execution of purpose, alignment strengthens.

Schedule regular "clarity reviews" with your leadership team to test whether your CPoP still resonates. Ask questions like:

- Who are we serving today?
- Has their biggest possibility or aspiration shifted?
- Does our CPoP still feel authentic, energizing, and memorable?

Involve employees, customers, and partners in this conversation. Their voices offer vital insight into how well your CPoP is connecting in the real world. When everyone understands, lives, and believes in the CPoP, your organization stays aligned and energized.

These periodic refreshes don't mean constantly rewriting where you're executing on your purpose, rather, they help you refine and sharpen it so that it continues to invite curiosity and inspire action. A refined CPoP should strengthen coherence across family and self, employees, customers, investors, and community rather than privileging one at the expense of another.

Remember, a powerful CPoP is the clearest expression of where you are executing on your purpose today. Keeping it fresh and relevant is one of the highest acts of credible leadership.

Building Accountability Rituals

Accountability is the glue that holds Executive Abundance together over time. Without it, even the best purpose statements and credibility systems can fade under daily pressures. Sustainable abundance requires consistent, repeatable practices that remind everyone of your shared commitments.

These rituals protect consistency and commitment across the EA Ecosystem. They ensure that clarity does not drift, credibility does not erode, and one stakeholder group is not unintentionally prioritized at the expense of another.

Establish simple rituals that keep your team focused on living the values of clarity, credibility, consistency, and commitment. For example:

- **Weekly reflections:** Briefly review how recent decisions or actions align with your CPoP.
- **Quarterly stakeholder trust audits:** Measure how each stakeholder group perceives your credibility and identify areas to strengthen.
- **Credibility storytelling:** Invite team members to share a moment when they witnessed credible behavior, helping to spread inspiration.

These rituals are more than checklists. They are opportunities to reconnect with your purpose and encourage an honest conversation about where you might be drifting off course.

Make these accountability processes visible, transparent, and team-owned. When employees feel they are part of maintaining the standard, they become active participants in sustaining Executive Abundance, not passive observers. When accountability becomes shared and structured, Executive Abundance no longer depends on a single leader's vigilance. It becomes embedded in how the organization operates.

A culture of accountability ensures your purpose stays alive, your values stay authentic, and your stakeholder trust grows stronger year after year.

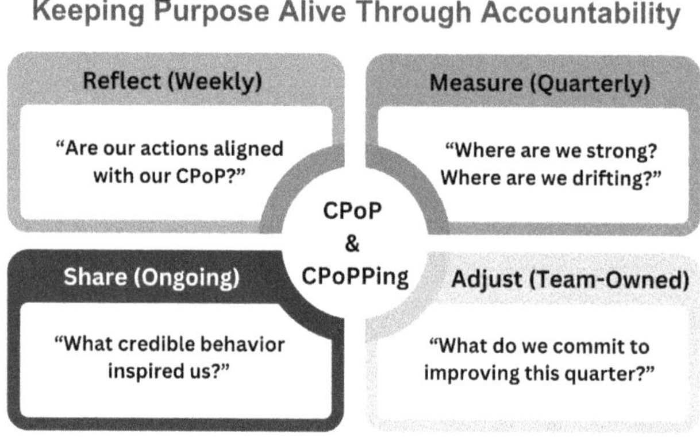

Figure 19: Keeping Purpose Alive Through Accountability

Maintaining Purpose Under Pressure

It is easy to live your purpose when things are going well; but the true test of Executive Abundance comes during periods of crisis, rapid growth, or uncertainty. Under pressure, leaders often revert to old habits, sacrificing long-term purpose for short-term survival.

Pressure does not always look the same. In crisis, the temptation is to compromise standards to survive. In rapid growth, the temptation is to stretch beyond your capacity and lose coherence. In long periods of stability, the temptation is to assume alignment will sustain itself without discipline. Each scenario requires conscious reinforcement of your commitments.

To resist this temptation, anchor your team to your values. Remind them that your CPoP and your 10 Credibility Values are not negotiable, even when challenges arise. In fact, those principles are most powerful precisely when the stakes are high.

Model vulnerability by being open about trade-offs and mistakes. When you lead transparently during difficult times, you build deeper trust with stakeholders. Let them see how you are balancing immediate needs with your commitment to sustained abundance.

Encourage your team to raise concerns if they see purpose drifting off course. Psychological safety is essential for maintaining values during stress. A healthy culture empowers everyone to protect the mission, not just the leadership.

Finally, celebrate the moments when you hold true to your purpose under pressure. These moments reinforce that your standards are systemic, not situational. When your team sees consistency under pressure, they learn that Executive Abundance is not dependent on circumstances or charisma, but on disciplined practice. These stories become part of your legacy and proof that Executive Abundance is not just an idea, but a durable, credible way of leading, no matter what challenges come your way.

Reflection and Action

Sustaining Executive Abundance requires vigilance, humility, and a commitment to keep evolving. Use these questions to reflect on how well you are building a long-term abundance practice:

- When was the last time we reviewed our CPoP for relevance and clarity?
- Are we regularly checking in on stakeholder trust and credibility?
- What rituals do we have in place to keep our CPoP front and center?
- How do we support our teams in maintaining purpose during stressful or uncertain times?

Micro-Commitment:

Choose one micro-commitment this week to reinforce your accountability and purpose. It might be:

- ☐ Scheduling a stakeholder trust audit.
- ☐ Revisiting your CPoP with your leadership team.
- ☐ Sharing a vulnerability moment with your employees.

Remember, Executive Abundance is a practice. Like any discipline, it stays alive only through consistent action and reflection. Sustaining your purpose, values, and credibility is what will transform Executive Abundance from a powerful idea into a permanent way of leading.

Summary

Executive Abundance is a lifelong practice, not a one-time initiative. In this chapter, you explored how to keep your CPoP relevant as your stakeholders and markets change, and how to build accountability rituals that help you stay aligned with your purpose and values. You also discovered how to maintain credibility under pressure by modeling vulnerability, transparency, and a commitment to stakeholder trust even during crises. Sustaining Executive Abundance requires consistent, credible habits that reinforce clarity, consistency, and commitment year after year, turning the execution of your purpose into a durable leadership legacy.

When these habits are embedded across your organization, Executive Abundance moves beyond individual leadership and becomes part of how the system operates.

AHAs

- **AHA #37:** *Abundance is a lifelong practice, not a quick fix.*
- **AHA #38:** *Consistency and accountability sustain trust over time.*
- **AHA #39:** *Purpose in action holds steady even as circumstances change.*

Chapter 14

Multiplying Executive Abundance Across the Leadership System

Introduction

Executive Abundance becomes durable when it extends beyond a single leader and takes root across the leadership system.

Sustaining alignment is essential. Multiplying it is transformational.

When clarity, credibility, consistency, and commitment are modeled only at the top, the organization remains personality-dependent. When those principles are distributed across managers, team leads, partners, and future successors, Executive Abundance becomes cultural rather than individual.

This chapter explores how to intentionally multiply the EA Engine across the EA Ecosystem so that alignment strengthens at every level. Mentoring matters. Modeling matters. But system design matters most.

Multiplication ensures that Executive Abundance holds not only across cycles of scarcity and success, but across leadership layers and time.

Developing Future Leaders of Abundance

Mentorship is more than transferring skills; it is transferring mindset, purpose, and values. If you want Executive Abundance to survive and thrive beyond your personal influence, you must intentionally develop leaders who share your commitment to leading with Executive Abundance.

Developing future leaders is not simply about succession planning. It is about distributing responsibility for clarity, credibility, consistency, and commitment across levels of leadership. When mid-level leaders understand how their decisions affect employees, customers, investors, and community, Executive Abundance begins to scale systemically.

Start by identifying individuals who show a passion for serving others, a willingness to learn, and the courage to lead with authenticity. These are the seeds of abundance-minded leadership.

Once identified, invest in them. Share your lessons, your stories of vulnerability, and your moments of triumph and failure. Model how you apply your CPoP and the 10 Credibility Values in everyday choices. Provide them with opportunities to lead, coach others, and take ownership of stakeholder trust initiatives.

Create intentional structures for this development. For example:

- Shadowing programs that let emerging leaders see purpose in action.
- Regular mentorship conversations that focus on values as well as strategy.
- Celebrating and rewarding credible, purpose-driven decisions.

Remember, your role is not to clone yourself but to help each future leader discover their authentic way of embodying Executive Abundance. When they feel empowered to lead with their own voice, aligned to the same core principles, your movement expands organically.

Spreading the 10 Credibility Values

For Executive Abundance to flourish, the 10 Credibility Values (see Chapter 4 or Appendix A) cannot remain abstract or reserved for a handful of top leaders, they must be woven into the entire organization. Mentorship is a powerful way to accomplish that.

Values become durable when they are embedded in hiring decisions, performance evaluations, promotion criteria, and leadership development pathways. When credibility is structurally reinforced, it survives leadership turnover and market shifts.

Use mentorship relationships to consistently emphasize these values: authenticity, integrity (both internal and external), vulnerability, coachability, servant leadership, intent, commitment, sharing your stage, and showing respect. Encourage mentees to explore what these values mean in practice, and invite them to share real-world stories of when they applied them or saw them in action.

Incorporate the Credibility Values into training, onboarding, and leadership development programs. Make them a living framework that shapes how people interact, solve problems, and make decisions. Celebrate and recognize credible behaviors publicly, reinforcing that these values are not a side conversation, they are the foundation of how you do business.

When new leaders see the Credibility Values rewarded, acknowledged, and discussed regularly, they will naturally adopt and protect them. Over time, these values become part of the cultural fabric, creating a powerful, self-reinforcing cycle of abundance.

Elevating Partners and Champions

Executive Abundance doesn't stop inside your organization. To truly multiply its impact, you need to elevate partners, community allies, and referral champions who share where you are executing on your purpose and your values.

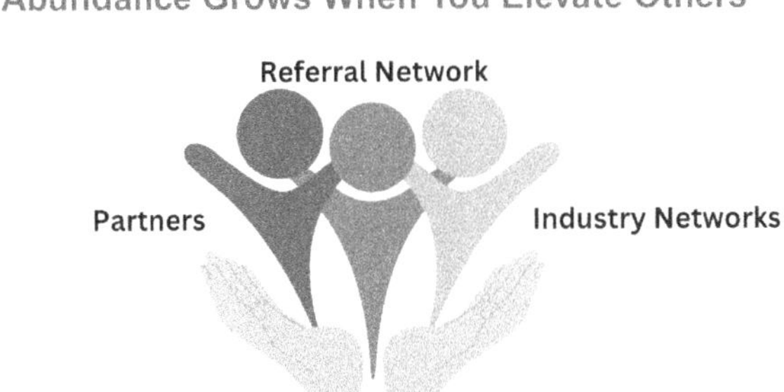

Figure 20: Abundance Grows When You Elevate Others

Partners and champions extend Executive Abundance beyond formal reporting lines. When aligned stakeholders reinforce your standards externally, the EA Ecosystem strengthens organically. Multiplication at the ecosystem level protects coherence even when internal leadership shifts.

Look for opportunities to co-create with these partners. Invite them into your initiatives, celebrate their successes, and give them a platform to tell their stories. By "sharing your stage," what I call spreading credust, you amplify their voices and create a positive cycle of trust, influence, and abundance.

Offer mentorship beyond your walls; for example, partnering with nonprofit boards, professional associations, or industry networks to build a culture of credible leadership at scale. Your influence as a mentor extends far when you help develop others who may not directly work for you, but who still align with your mission and values.

These partners become extensions of your legacy. They bring your principles to new audiences, industries, and communities, expanding the ripple effect of Executive Abundance far beyond what you alone could achieve.

When you elevate others authentically, you shift from being a solitary leader to a true ecosystem builder, someone who creates space for abundance to thrive everywhere.

Reflection and Action

Multiplication is one of the most powerful ways to build a legacy. To multiply Executive Abundance across the leadership system, you must continually invest in developing other credible, purpose-driven leaders. Use these questions to reflect on how you can start today:

- Who in my network shows the potential to be an abundance-minded leader?
- How can I intentionally share my CPoP and Credibility Values with them?
- Where could I co-create opportunities for partners and community champions to lead?
- Am I rewarding and celebrating credible, purpose-driven choices across my ecosystem?

Micro-Commitment:

Choose one micro-commitment this week to expand your influence by multiplying Executive Abundance. It might be:

- ☐ Having a values-focused conversation with a rising leader.
- ☐ Offering to coach a community partner.
- ☐ Recognizing someone who exemplifies credible leadership.

Remember, multiplying Executive Abundance is how you transform it from a single voice into a movement, one that echoes through future generations of leaders.

Summary

Multiplying Executive Abundance across the leadership system expands impact beyond a single leader. In this chapter, you explored how to identify and develop future leaders who share your commitment to the EA Engine. You learned how to spread the 10 Credibility Values through structured programs, storytelling, and day-to-day leadership, and how to elevate community partners and referral champions to extend where you are executing on your purpose beyond your walls. When you invest in growing other credible, purpose-driven leaders, you build a legacy that expands far beyond what you alone could accomplish, turning Executive Abundance into a true movement.

AHAs

- **AHA #40:** *What you scale becomes your culture.*
- **AHA #41:** *Your legacy grows when you elevate others.*
- **AHA #42:** *Credibility shared is credibility multiplied.*

Chapter 15

What You Reinforce Becomes Your Legacy

Introduction

Figure 21: Stakeholder Success

This powerful idea captures the true measure of Executive Abundance. Your legacy is not about trophies, titles, or personal wealth. It is about what you consistently reinforce.

Over time, what you measure, reward, protect, and correct shapes the experience others have of you. It shapes culture. It shapes decisions. It shapes outcomes.

When your stakeholders (family and self, employees, customers, investors, and community) succeed because of the standards you consistently reinforce, your influence continues long after you are gone. That is the ultimate expression of Executive Abundance: building systems, habits, and cultures that empower others to reach their possibilities.

In this chapter, you will explore how to define, measure, and intentionally build this kind of leadership legacy. You'll reflect on how to capture lessons and stories that matter, and how to sustain a purpose-driven impact that grows beyond your own direct involvement.

Finally, I will share how you can partner with me if you want guidance to embed Executive Abundance deeply and leave a legacy that truly matters.

Defining Your Legacy

Your legacy deserves to be intentional, not accidental. It is easy to think of legacy as something to consider at the end of a career, but truly credible leaders define it while they are still actively leading. That way, every decision, conversation, and action moves you closer to the story you want others to tell about you.

Intentional legacy is not defined by aspiration alone. It is defined by reinforcement. The standards you consistently uphold, the behaviors you reward, and the shortcuts you refuse to tolerate quietly shape how others experience your leadership.

Ask yourself:

- What do I want people to say about me when I'm not in the room?
- How do I want my stakeholders (family and self, employees, customers, investors, community) to feel because of how I showed up?
- What impact do I want to be whispered behind my back?

Remember, "The legacy of a leader is felt in the success of their stakeholders." Your legacy is ultimately measured by the growth, empowerment, and well-being of those you consistently elevate.

Document your vision of legacy clearly. Write down how you want to influence each stakeholder group, what positive ripple effects you hope to create, and what values you refuse to compromise. Treat this as a living declaration that can evolve as your purpose grows and the world changes.

By defining your legacy now, you create a powerful compass that guides you through both triumphs and challenges, keeping your Executive Abundance focused on what truly matters.

Measuring and Celebrating Impact

Legacy is not measured by what you intend to do but by what actually happens because of you. If you want your Executive Abundance to endure, you must measure its impact in meaningful ways, beyond revenue or growth targets. What you choose to measure signals what matters. Over time, those signals shape behavior across the leadership system.

Think about metrics that reveal how your stakeholders are thriving:

- Are you, and your family, experiencing greater well-being and purpose?
- Are your employees more fulfilled and engaged?
- Are your customers more loyal and trusting?
- Are your investors seeing sustainable, long-term value?
- Is your community benefiting from your presence and contribution?

Collect stories, testimonials, and examples of transformation. These become proof points of your purpose in action and can inspire others to carry your mission forward.

Also, celebrate these outcomes. Recognition is a powerful way to reinforce your legacy. When you consistently recognize clarity, credibility, consistency, and commitment in action, you strengthen the EA Engine across the entire ecosystem. Celebrate stakeholder success generously; highlight teams, individuals, and partners who make Executive Abundance real. When you shine a light on the success of others, spreading credust, your own leadership legacy grows even stronger.

Remember, your impact is best measured by the lives you elevate, not just the bottom line. That is how Executive Abundance lives on.

Sustaining the Journey

Executive Abundance is not a finish line, it is a lifelong journey. Once you have defined your legacy and started measuring its impact, the next challenge is sustaining it over time, even as circumstances shift.

Circumstances will shift through cycles of scarcity, success, and stability. Sustaining Executive Abundance requires reinforcing your standards in each condition, not just when momentum is on your side.

The Lifelong Journey of Leadership

Abundance is not a destination: it's a rhythm of purpose, service, and gratitude.

Figure 22: The Lifelong Journey of Leadership

First, build support systems that keep you grounded. Surround yourself with mentors, peer communities, and accountability partners who will remind you of your purpose in action when distractions or pressures tempt you to compromise.

Continue to invest in your own growth. Personal growth matters, but systems matter more. The habits and structures you build must continue reinforcing alignment even when your direct presence is absent. Leadership demands constant learning, and abundance-minded leaders must stay open to new ideas, new perspectives, and emerging stakeholder needs. That flexibility keeps your legacy alive and relevant.

Encourage those you mentor to carry the mission forward, multiplying your influence. Share your stories, lessons, and wisdom so they can adapt Executive Abundance to their own style while honoring its core values.

Finally, remember to practice gratitude. Recognizing the opportunities, people, and communities who helped you lead abundantly will keep you humble and inspired to continue the work. Gratitude fuels consistency and renews your commitment to the path.

When you sustain your journey with purpose, curiosity, gratitude, and disciplined reinforcement, your Executive Abundance becomes embedded in culture and lives on in every life you elevate.

Invitation to Partner

If you are ready to embed Executive Abundance more deeply into your leadership system, I would be honored to support that work.

Over the years, I have helped leaders clarify where they are executing on their purpose through their CPoP and align clarity, credibility, consistency, and commitment across their organizations. Embedding the EA Engine across the EA Ecosystem requires discipline, structure, and honest reflection. It is meaningful work.

Whether you are looking to:

- Align your executive leadership team around a shared CPoP and stakeholder coherence.
- Strengthen credibility practices across your organization.
- Build operating rhythms that sustain alignment across cycles of scarcity and success.

If this next step would serve you, you can connect with me directly at MitchellLevy.com, email me at mitchell.levy@gmail.com, or call (+1) 408-257-3000.

Executive Abundance is sustained through reinforcement. If you choose to deepen that practice, I would be honored to walk alongside you.

Reflection and Action

As you look ahead to reinforcing Executive Abundance every day, take time to reflect on these essential questions:

- What do I want my legacy to be, in simple, human words?
- How will I know if my stakeholders are truly thriving because of my leadership?
- Which systems, habits, or rituals can I build to keep my legacy authentic and consistent?
- Who can I mentor or partner with to extend my purpose beyond myself?

If you consistently apply what you've learned in these pages, you already have what you need to build a lasting leadership legacy.

Micro-Commitment:

Choose one micro-commitment today that reinforces the legacy you want to build:

- ☐ Sharing your story with a team.
- ☐ Asking a trusted peer for feedforward on how you show up.
- ☐ Revisiting your CPoP with fresh eyes.

Your Executive Abundance is too important to leave to chance. Small, consistent actions rooted in clarity, credibility, consistency, and commitment will shape how others experience your leadership. That is legacy built through reinforcement.

Summary

Legacy is not built at the end of your career. It is built through what you consistently reinforce.

In this chapter, you explored how to define your leadership legacy not as intention, but as lived experience. You examined how stakeholder success becomes the clearest evidence of Executive Abundance, and how measuring, celebrating, and sustaining that success strengthens clarity, credibility, consistency, and commitment over time.

You were also invited to consider how embedding Executive Abundance across your leadership system protects that legacy across cycles and transitions. Ultimately, a leader's legacy is measured by the sustained success of their stakeholders.

AHAs

- **AHA #43:** *Legacy is how your purpose in action lives on.*
- **AHA #44:** *Measure impact by the lives you touch, not just profits.*
- **AHA #45:** *Your Executive Abundance becomes your legacy when it is consistently reinforced.*

Conclusion

The Future of Executive Abundance Starts with You

The world needs leaders who are clear, credible, consistent, and committed. Leaders who build trust across family and self, employees, customers, investors, and community. Leaders who understand that success is sustained through disciplined alignment.

Executive Abundance is not a moment. It is not a slogan. It is not a finish line.

- It is clarity reinforced.
- It is credibility practiced.
- It is consistency embedded.
- It is commitment sustained.

Over time, what you reinforce becomes culture. Culture shapes decisions. Decisions shape how your stakeholders experience you. When your stakeholders thrive because of your leadership, your legacy endures.

Executive Abundance will not be defined by theory. It will be defined by leaders who choose, daily, to live it.

It starts with what you reinforce.

It starts with the next decision you make.

Afterword by Dr. Marshall Goldsmith For *Executive Abundance*

When I first met Mitchell Levy, what stood out most was his deep desire to help leaders become better versions of themselves. He has always been less interested in titles and more interested in impact. Over the years, I have watched him coach, listen, learn, and refine his understanding of what truly creates meaningful leadership.

Executive Abundance represents the culmination of those years of work. Mitchell has taken thousands of data points, countless coaching conversations, and a lifetime of service and distilled them into a framework that is as human as it is practical. Clarity, credibility, consistency, and commitment: these are the behaviors that shape a leader's legacy. They determine whether people trust us, whether organizations grow, and whether our lives align with what we say matters most.

Leaders often ask me, "When will I have it all figured out?"

My answer is always the same: "Never."

Leadership is not about achieving perfection. It is about practicing the right behaviors every day, involving the people around us, and making life a little better for those we serve. Mitchell's work reminds us of that truth.

As you close this book, I hope you feel inspired not just to think differently, but to act differently. Your leadership will be defined not by what you know, but by the choices you make from this moment forward. May this book help you choose well.

— Dr. Marshall Goldsmith
Thinkers50 #1 Executive Coach and New York Times bestselling author of The Earned Life, Triggers, and What Got You Here Won't Get You There

Afterword by Maynard Webb

I've been a CEO, a board chair, and a board member and the founder of a firm that invests in early-stage startups. I've operated companies through rapid growth, managed turnarounds, and been in rooms where we had to make high-stakes decisions with incomplete information that had real consequences for employees, customers, and shareholders.

What I've learned in my 40-year career in tech is that leadership rarely fails because people don't care or don't work hard enough. It fails when the pace of pressure outstrips a team's ability to stay aligned on what matters.

That pressure isn't new, but its intensity is. Leaders today are managing quarterly expectations, real-time performance metrics, investor narratives, social media amplification, and internal execution demands—all at once. The expectation is that you'll be decisive, transparent, empathetic, and consistent, often in the same moment. It's a tall order.

That's what Mitchell Levy tackles in this book. He calls it Executive Abundance. I call it "the spirit of And." Whatever you call it, doing more requires something deeper than speed or optimization. It requires clarity and alignment.

I appreciate that Mitchell's framework doesn't treat leadership as a checklist of virtues. He addresses it as an interconnected system built to hold under pressure. He shows how clarity requires credibility, and credibility requires consistency, and all of it requires real commitment. I've seen this in every organization I've been a part of—you are earning or losing credibility every day.

I know Mitchell through our time at Bay Networks. It's great to see him codify decades of leadership insight across his books and coaching practice. What he presents here comes from sustained engagement with real leadership challenges, not theory developed at a distance. The value is that he's given leaders a disciplined way to think about maintaining integrity when things get gnarly—or as he might say, when conditions aren't ideal and trade-offs are unavoidable.

In my time as an operator and an advisor I've seen how easily individuals and teams can mistake action for traction. The strength of this book is that it takes obligations seriously. It illustrates that leaders are accountable to employees, customers, investors, communities, and their own sustainability. Ignoring any one of those dimensions doesn't simplify the job but increases risk. *Executive Abundance* offers a way to preserve what matters without losing momentum.

This book is not a prescription; it's a lens. Use it to see the systems you're operating within and make more deliberate choices about how you are going to show up and contribute. And see it as I do—evidence that we're all capable of more when we approach leadership as a system and a service.

— Maynard Webb
Board Member, Salesforce, Visa and AppLovin; former CEO LiveOps; former COO, eBay

Author's Note

Thank you for investing your time, energy, and trust in exploring Executive Abundance with me. It is my deepest belief that leadership is one of the most powerful forces for good on this planet… when it is rooted in clarity, credibility, consistency, and commitment.

As you move forward, remember that Executive Abundance is not a destination but a way of being, expressed every day through how you show up for yourself, your team, your customers, your investors, and your community. This book is not meant to be rushed or mastered. It is meant to be practiced, reflected on, and returned to as your leadership context evolves.

Executive Abundance was developed as part of a doctoral capstone examining how leaders behave under sustained performance pressure.

If you ever feel stuck, unsure, or simply want to share how these ideas have helped you, I encourage you to reach out. I would be honored to hear your story and support your next steps.

You can always connect with me directly:
MitchellLevy.com
mitchell.levy@gmail.com
(+1) 408-257-3000

Your journey matters. Your legacy matters. And the world needs your Executive Abundance now more than ever.

With gratitude,
Dr. Mitchell Levy

About the Author

Dr. Mitchell Levy is a Global Credibility Expert, executive coach, and author of more than 60 books. A two-time TEDx speaker and international bestselling author, he has spent decades helping executives and organizations align purpose with performance.

Over the course of his career, Dr. Levy has interviewed more than 500 global leaders to understand what makes individuals and organizations truly Trusted, Known, and Liked, and why so many struggle to sustain that credibility under pressure.

His Executive Abundance Framework integrates decades of applied leadership experience with doctoral research in Transformation Leadership and Organizational Change. The framework equips leaders to create clarity, build trust, and generate enduring value across cycles of scarcity and success.

Dr. Levy has guided more than 1,000 executives and organizations in articulating their authentic value through their CPoP (Customer Point of Possibilities), and embedding that purpose into daily leadership decisions.

Learn more at MitchellLevy.com.

Appendix A

The 10 Credibility Values: Quick Reference Guide

This appendix supports the Credibility component of the EA Engine. Use this guide to check yourself, coach your teams, and inspire your stakeholders to live and lead with greater trust, clarity, and purpose.

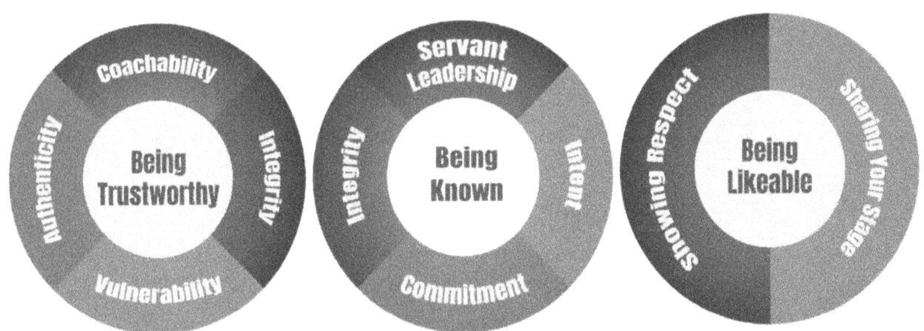

Values associated with Being Trusted:

1. Coachability
Stay open to learning, adapting, and evolving with fresh insights from others.

2. External Integrity
Clearly define and communicate who you claim to be, including the values and commitments you publicly stand behind.

3. Vulnerability
Be willing to show humility, admit mistakes, and invite feedforward, even when it feels uncomfortable.

4. Authenticity
Be real and genuine in all your interactions, showing up with honesty and transparency.

Values associated with Being Known:

5. Servant Leadership

Lead by putting the needs of others first, empowering and uplifting those you serve.

6. Intent to Do the Right Thing

Approach every decision with a genuine desire to create positive outcomes for your stakeholders.

7. Commitment to Do the Right Thing

Act on that intent with courage, consistency, and follow-through.

8. Internal Integrity

Demonstrate alignment between who you say you are and who you are in private, especially when no one is watching.

Values associated with Being Liked:

9. Respect

Treat everyone with dignity, empathy, and kindness, regardless of status or circumstance.

10. Sharing Your Stage (AKA Sharing Credust)

Elevate others by spotlighting their contributions and giving credit freely, sharing your platform is sharing your credibility.

Appendix B

The EA Clarity Roadmap

The EA Clarity Roadmap is a practical four-step tool that supports the Clarity and Credibility components of the EA Engine. Use this roadmap to keep your organization and leadership aligned with where you execute on your purpose.

EA Clarity Roadmap

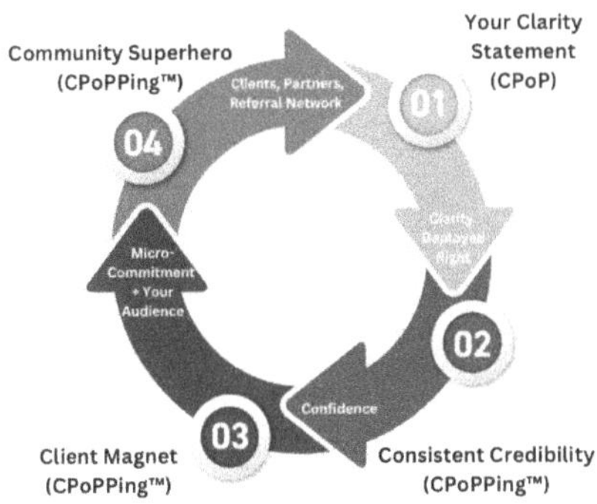

1. Your Clarity Statement (CPoP)

- Craft a concise, memorable statement (3-9 words) that describes who you serve and what possibility you help them achieve.
- Your CPoP is where you are executing on your purpose today.

2. Consistent Credibility (CPoPping™)

- Ensure that your actions, messages, and behaviors align with your CPoP.
- Show up authentically and consistently across every touchpoint, both synchronously and asynchronously.

3. Client Magnet

- Offer a micro-commitment product or service that allows your audience to experience your credibility and purpose in action before they fully engage.
- This might be a workshop, free resource, or introductory program that demonstrates trustworthiness and value.

4. Community Superhero

- Build a network of clients, partners, and champions who will recommend you.
- Strengthen your referral network by consistently living your CPoP and delivering on your promises.

Appendix C

EA Ecosystem Alignment Review

Use this audit tool to assess how well Executive Abundance is holding across the five EA Ecosystem stakeholder groups. Review these questions regularly (quarterly is ideal) to stay accountable to your purpose in action and credibility.

Stakeholder Group 1: Family and Self

- Am I prioritizing my personal well-being and sense of purpose?
- Do I feel aligned with my own values?
- How am I investing in my growth and fulfillment?

Stakeholder Group 2: Employees

- Do our employees understand and connect with our CPoP?
- Am I modeling credibility consistently for them?
- How well am I listening to their needs and empowering their success?

Stakeholder Group 3: Customers

- Are our customers experiencing our purpose in action?
- Do they trust us to deliver on our promises?
- What is the level of their loyalty, and how are we measuring it?

Stakeholder Group 4: Investors

- Are we providing authentic, sustainable value to our investors?
- How do our long-horizon strategies reflect Executive Abundance?
- Am I communicating transparently about our successes and challenges?

The EA Ecosystem

Stakeholder Group 5: Community (Physical & Virtual)

- Are we showing up consistently and authentically for our community partners?
- Do they see our credibility and purpose demonstrated through our actions?
- How am I investing in relationships and partnerships that uplift the broader EA ecosystem?

Appendix D

EA Ecosystem Micro-Commitments Under Pressure

Small, consistent actions reinforce Executive Abundance over time. Use these EA Ecosystem micro-commitments to reinforce clarity, credibility, consistency, and commitment across stakeholder groups when pressure tempts you to narrow your focus.

For Family and Self:

- Block 15 minutes each week to reflect on your CPoP.
- Schedule one vulnerability conversation with a trusted peer.
- Write down one value-driven decision you made each day.

For Employees:

- Recognize an employee who demonstrated a credibility value.
- Invite an employee to share their own purpose in a team meeting.
- Host a "credibility storytelling" lunch once a month.

For Customers:

- Share a behind-the-scenes story showing your values in action.
- Personally thank one loyal customer each week.
- Ask a customer for honest feedforward on how you deliver purpose.

For Investors:

- Provide a transparent quarterly update beyond the numbers.
- Invite investors to a conversation about long-horizon, purpose-driven goals.
- Share how your values have shaped a key strategic choice.

For Community:

- Promote a partner or community initiative on your platform.
- Attend one local or virtual event to support community building.
- Highlight a community member's contribution in your newsletter or online.

Here's my tip:

- Pick one micro-commitment each week and build from there. Executive Abundance grows through small, steady steps.

Appendix E

Running an EA Clarity Session

A Clarity Session is a structured, high-impact conversation designed to help individuals or teams define where they are executing on their purpose, their CPoP (Customer Point of Possibilities). This is not a brainstorming meeting. It's a focused dialogue that strips away fluff and gets to the heart of who you serve and the specific possibility you unlock for them.

These sessions are essential whether you're an individual leader seeking deeper clarity or a leadership team trying to align your message, direction, and purpose-driven actions.

Core Objectives of a Clarity Session

- Identify the audience you serve most powerfully.
- Articulate the specific outcome or transformation they seek.
- Distill that insight into a CPoP, 3-9 words.
- Use the CPoP as both a compass (to guide internal decisions) and a magnet (to attract aligned stakeholders and opportunities).

Lay the groundwork for operationalizing the CPoP. I call this CPoPping™.

Suggested Format

- Timeframe: 60–90 minutes (for individuals or small teams).
- Ideal Participants: Key decision-makers, brand owners, culture champions.
- Facilitator Tip: It helps to have someone external or neutral facilitate so all voices can be heard.

Session Outline

1. Opening Intention (5-10 minutes)

- Share the goal of the session: to define where you're executing on your purpose *right now*, not where you aspire to be.
- Reinforce the value of radical clarity; how it connects to credibility, trust, and alignment.

2. Stakeholder Reflection (10-15 minutes)

- Who are your core customer stakeholders?
- Where are you making the greatest impact today?
- Which group do you serve best (revenue, results, alignment)?

Prompt: "If 80% of your success comes from one audience, who are they?" or "Where do you feel most alive and valuable in your work?"

3. Possibility Discovery (15-20 minutes)

- What aspiration or result does that audience truly care about?
- What outcome do they seek that you consistently help deliver?
- Push beyond features. Focus on the transformation or relief you enable.

Prompt: "What are your clients really buying, not the service itself, but the change?" or "What future are you making possible for them?"

4. Drafting the CPoP (15-20 minutes)

- Use this format: [Audience or Client Group] + [Aspirational Outcome or Problem Solved]
- Keep it 3-9 words.
- It must spark curiosity and pass the "tell me more" test.

Examples:

- "Tech Leaders Scaling Trust in Turbulent Markets."
- "Purpose-Driven Founders Growing without Burnout."
- "Nonprofits Amplifying their Donor Impact."

Let the group generate a few versions, then test aloud: "Would this spark a 'tell me more'?" or "Would our clients feel seen by this?"

5. Testing and Feedback (10-15 minutes)

- Share potential CPoPs with outside stakeholders, internal teams, or trusted advisors.
- Ask:
  - Is it clear?
  - Is it memorable?
  - Is it relevant?
  - Does it feel like you?
  - Do you want to know more?

Final Tips

- Don't let "perfect" be the enemy of the powerful. Your CPoP can and will evolve.
- Keep refining until it's easy to say, easy to share, and makes people lean in.
- Use it every day and it will evolve into a living magnet for the right opportunities.
- If you want virtual help from Dr. Levy with with your CPoP, visit The CPoP Architect at: https://aha.pub/TheCPoPArchitect.

Appendix F

Running an Accountability Mondays Operating Rhythm

Accountability Mondays are a simple, high-trust operating rhythm designed to keep individuals and teams aligned with their CPoP (Customer Point of Possibilities) and consistently executing with clarity and credibility. This rhythm strengthens the Consistency and Commitment components of the EA Engine by reinforcing alignment week after week.

Whether you're a solopreneur, executive, or leading a team of 10,000, Accountability Mondays ground your focus, prevent drift, and translate purpose in action into disciplined action.

Purpose of the Session

1. Keep your CPoP top of mind every week.
2. Align weekly priorities with where you're executing on your purpose.
3. Identify misalignments or distractions before they derail progress.
4. Build a culture of ownership, trust, and micro-commitments.

Suggested Format

- Timeframe: 15–30 minutes.
- Frequency: Weekly (Monday mornings are ideal, but you can adapt).
- Participants: Self, teams, departments, or executive leadership groups.
- Tools: Journal, team dashboard, or shared doc.

Session Flow

1. Start with the CPoP (1–2 minutes per person)

Begin every session by re-stating your CPoP out loud. If it's a team, have someone different say it each week. After a 1-2 second pause, follow the CPoP by the 30–60 second tell-me-more.

"Let's start with a reminder of where we're executing on purpose right now … "

This practice reinforces shared clarity and signals that everything that follows must align.

2. Celebrate Credible Progress (5–10 minutes)

Share one example of how your actions last week lived the CPoP:

- A decision that reflected your purpose.
- A conversation that reinforced your values.
- A piece of content or interaction that sparked a "tell me more."

Prompt: "Where did you show up credibly last week?" or "What action reinforced trust, made you more known, or strengthened likability?"

This helps build a habit of credibility awareness and self-reflection.

3. Plan Purpose-Aligned Actions (5-10 minutes)

Ask:

- What are your top 1–3 priorities this week?
- How do they align with your CPoP?
- What micro-commitment will help you move the needle?

Prompt: "What is one action you'll take this week that directly supports our CPoP?" or "What stakeholder group will feel the impact?"

4. Surface Gaps or Misalignments (5 minutes)

Briefly invite team members (or yourself) to reflect:

- Where did we drift from our purpose?
- What feels out of sync?
- Where might we be overpromising and underdelivering?

This creates a safe, regular space to catch and correct alignment issues before they compound.

Tips for Leaders

- Model vulnerability: Share your own missteps or learnings. That builds trust.
- Don't let it become rote: Keep it real, fresh, and tied to outcomes.
- Make it shareable: Use highlights in newsletters, Slack, or 1x1s.

Why It Works

Accountability Mondays are about building the habit of alignment. When people consistently align their actions with purpose, week after week, clarity sharpens, credibility deepens, consistency stabilizes, and commitment strengthens. They become more trusted, more known, and more liked, not by force, but by showing up authentically and clearly. That's the essence of Executive Abundance.

Appendix G

Key AHAs from Each Chapter

Each AHA highlights a key insight from its chapter. Together, they map the journey from personal leadership clarity to lasting Executive Abundance across the five stakeholder groups.

Part 1: The Abundance Imperative: Why Traditional Success Metrics Fall Short

Chapter 1: Credibility Crisis: The Invisible Force Behind It

- **AHA #1:** *In today's world, credibility is the currency of leadership. Without it, trust collapses.*
- **AHA #2:** *Credibility is no longer just about being believed; it's about being Trusted, Known, and Liked.*
- **AHA #3:** *Authentic leaders align what they project with how they act, even when no one is watching.*

Chapter 2: Redefining Success: What We Reinforce Shapes What We Become

- **AHA #4:** *True success is measured in the positive impact you have on all stakeholders, not just your bottom line.*
- **AHA #5:** *Executive Abundance is not a tactic, it's a philosophy of leadership rooted in clarity, credibility, consistency, and commitment.*
- **AHA #6:** *A leader's legacy is whispered behind their back, and felt in the thriving success of those they serve.*

Part 2: The EA Engine: Clarity, Credibility, Consistency, and Commitment

Chapter 3: Clarity: Defining Direction Through Your CPoP

- **AHA #7:** *Radical clarity attracts trust faster than any marketing trick.*
- **AHA #8:** *A CPoP is not what you do, it's the possibility you unlock.*
- **AHA #9:** *If your team can't explain your purpose in 3-9 words, they can't live it.*

Chapter 4: Credibility: Being Trusted, Being Known, and Being Liked

- **AHA #10:** *Credibility gives your purpose in action permission to be heard.*
- **AHA #11:** *Trust is built in actions, not announcements.*
- **AHA #12:** *Being trusted, known, and liked is not a bonus, it is a baseline.*

Chapter 5: Consistency: Protecting Trust Through Pattern Integrity

- **AHA #13:** *Consistency is the silent engine of trust.*
- **AHA #14:** *Operational credibility turns values into action.*
- **AHA #15:** *When clarity and credibility meet consistency, your CPoP becomes unstoppable.*

Chapter 6: Commitment: Sustaining Priorities Under Pressure

- **AHA #16:** *Commitment is where your CPoP meets practice.*
- **AHA #17:** *Consistency without commitment is just routine.*
- **AHA #18:** *Purpose in action is the highest credibility signal you can give.*

Part 3: The EA Ecosystem: Family and Self, Employees, Customers, Investors, and Community

Chapter 7: Family and Self: The Internal Operating System of Leadership

- **AHA #19:** *Executive Abundance begins with personal abundance.*
- **AHA #20:** *You cannot pour from an empty cup. Lead yourself first.*
- **AHA #21:** *How you show up at home for your family and yourself shapes how you show up at work.*

Chapter 8: Employees: The Organizational Operating System

- **AHA #22:** *Employees are a core stakeholder group within the Executive Abundance Ecosystem.*
- **AHA #23:** *Credibility is contagious; model it, and employees will live it.*
- **AHA #24:** *Culture is built one credible action at a time.*

Chapter 9: Customers: The External Test of Internal Alignment

- **AHA #25:** *Customers remember consistent credible experiences, not empty promises.*
- **AHA #26:** *Trust is the foundation of every customer partnership.*
- **AHA #27:** *Consistency is the hidden hero of customer loyalty.*

Chapter 10: Investors: Defending Long-Horizon Value Creation

- **AHA #28:** *Investors follow leaders who invest in people first.*
- **AHA #29:** *Trust flows from employees to customers to investors.*
- **AHA #30:** *Authenticity and stakeholder alignment build sustainable growth.*

Chapter 11: Community: Extending Credibility Beyond the Enterprise

- **AHA #31:** *Communities amplify your purpose in action beyond profit.*
- **AHA #32:** *Referral partners accelerate trust faster than any cold campaign.*
- **AHA #33:** *Credibility compounds when you serve society as well as business.*

Part 4: Executive Abundance Under Pressure: Coherence in Practice

Chapter 12: Executive Abundance Under Pressure: 10 Cases of Sustained Coherence

- **AHA #34:** *Clarity is a force multiplier.*
- **AHA #35:** *Credibility is earned through consistent behavior.*
- **AHA #36:** *Purpose in action becomes real when it shows up in systems, not just speeches.*

Part 5: Sustaining Executive Abundance Across Cycles

Chapter 13: Sustaining Executive Abundance: Embedding Alignment Into Operating Rhythm

- **AHA #37:** *Abundance is a lifelong practice, not a quick fix.*
- **AHA #38:** *Consistency and accountability sustain trust over time.*
- **AHA #39:** *Purpose in action holds steady even as circumstances change.*

Chapter 14: Multiplying Executive Abundance Across the Leadership System

- **AHA #40:** *What you scale becomes your culture.*
- **AHA #41:** *Your legacy grows when you elevate others.*
- **AHA #42:** *Credibility shared is credibility multiplied.*

Chapter 15: What You Reinforce Becomes Your Legacy

- **AHA #43:** *Legacy is how your purpose in action lives on.*
- **AHA #44:** *Measure impact by the lives you touch, not just profits.*
- **AHA #45:** *Your Executive Abundance becomes your legacy when it is consistently reinforced.*

Appendix H

Glossary of Terms

Abundance: A sustained condition of wholeness, trust, and forward momentum that arises when people and systems are aligned around meaningful purpose. Abundance is not excess or accumulation; it is the experience of sufficiency, health, and shared progress across life, work, and relationships.

Accountability Mondays: A recurring operating rhythm where individuals and teams reflect on how their priorities and actions align with their CPoP while reinforcing clarity, credibility, consistency, and commitment.

AHAs: Short, memorable insights found throughout the book that encapsulate key lessons of Executive Abundance. Each AHA is designed to spark reflection and action.

Being Liked: One of the three pillars of credibility. It refers to showing respect, empathy, and humanity in leadership; sharing the spotlight, building rapport, and treating others with dignity and care.

Being Known: The second pillar of credibility. Being Known means people authentically understand who you are, what you stand for, and how you consistently serve. It is earned through meaningful, repeated interactions, not surface visibility.

Being Trusted: The first pillar of credibility. Being Trusted means delivering on your promises, showing consistency in values and actions, and earning belief through integrity and vulnerability.

Client Magnet: The third step in the EA Clarity Roadmap. It refers to the moment when a stakeholder self-selects into your ecosystem through a micro-commitment, typically after connecting with your clarity and credibility.

Community Superhero: The fourth step in the EA Clarity Roadmap. When you consistently deliver on your purpose, clients and partners naturally become advocates, referring you and extending your impact through word of mouth.

Consistent Credibility: The second step in the EA Clarity Roadmap. It's about synchronously and asynchronously demonstrating where you're executing on your purpose, every day, in every interaction.

CPoP (Customer Point of Possibilities): A concise three to nine word statement that clarifies who you serve and the problem they want solved or the outcome they seek. A CPoP expresses where an individual or organization executes on their purpose through service to others.

CPoP-in-Action: The visible, lived execution of a leader's or organization's CPoP, demonstrated consistently through decisions, behaviors, systems, and culture.

CPoPping™: The continuous process of living your CPoP in both synchronous (conversations, meetings) and asynchronous (content, systems) ways. It's how credibility becomes visible and repeatable.

Credibility: Redefined in Dr. Levy's work as *the quality of being Trusted, Known, and Liked.* It is the bridge between stated purpose and perceived trustworthiness.

Credibility Compass: Your CPoP functions as a compass, helping guide internal decisions and behaviors in alignment with your purpose and values.

Credibility Magnet: Your CPoP also acts as a magnet, attracting aligned people, opportunities, and conversations that resonate with your clearly stated purpose.

Credibility Values: The set of leadership values that guide behavior and reinforce trust, visibility, and respect across relationships.

Credust™: A blend of credibility and trust. It reflects the goodwill and trust you receive when others share their platform or speak positively on your behalf, earned by consistently demonstrating trustworthiness and value.

Cultural Drift: The gradual misalignment that occurs when small compromises accumulate and reinforcement weakens over time.

EA Clarity Roadmap: A four-step process for strengthening the Clarity component of the EA Engine through articulation, visibility, and consistent execution:

1. Your Clarity Statement (CPoP).
2. Consistent Credibility (CPoPping™).
3. Client Magnet (CPoPping).
4. Community Superhero (CPoPping).

EA Ecosystem: The ordered and interdependent network of relationships through which Executive Abundance is experienced and sustained across five stakeholder groups: family and self, employees, customers, investors, and community.

EA Engine: The four interdependent leadership components of Executive Abundance: clarity, credibility, consistency, and commitment.

EA Framework: The integration of the EA Engine and the EA Ecosystem. It describes how leadership performance must operate consistently across stakeholder groups to sustain Executive Abundance.

Execution of Purpose: Execution of Purpose is the structural and strategic deployment of the CPoP across systems, processes, and teams. It goes beyond individual behaviors and ensures that how your organization operates consistently reflects why it exists.

Executive Abundance™: A governing leadership framework in which the interdependent component of the EA Engine: clarity, credibility, consistency, and commitment is intentionally applied across the EA Ecosystem of five interdependent stakeholder groups: family and self, employees, customers, investors, and community. Executive Abundance measures success by the sustained, trusted value created across this ecosystem through purpose in action.

Feedforward: A practice originated by Marshall Goldsmith that focuses on future improvement rather than past mistakes. Instead of traditional feedback, which looks backward, feedforward emphasizes constructive suggestions about what can be done differently going forward.

Five Stakeholder Groups: The five ordered and interdependent groups of the EA Ecosystem family and self, employees, customers, investors, and community. Strength at one level reinforces the next.

Leader's Legacy: A leaders legacy is felt by the success of their stakeholders.

Legacy: What people say about you when you're not in the room.

Micro-Commitment: A small, low-risk action taken by a stakeholder (like giving feedback or signing up for a resource) that begins the relationship-building journey. It is often sparked by a leader's clarity and credibility.

Operational Credibility: The embodiment of stated values and purpose within the actual operations, systems, and behaviors of an organization. It ensures alignment between external messaging and internal reality.

Purpose in Action: When a leader or organization doesn't just talk about purpose; they live it through consistent, meaningful, and credible behaviors that can be felt by stakeholders.

Radical Clarity: The unmistakable, purpose-driven expression of who you serve and what possibility you unlock. It instills confidence, invites trust, and becomes a magnetic force that aligns employees, customers, investors, and communities around a shared vision.

Reflection and Action: A section at the end of each chapter designed to prompt readers to apply the concepts. It includes reflection questions and a recommended micro-commitment to put ideas into motion.

Trust in Action: The visible and consistent demonstration of integrity, reliability, and alignment between words and deeds. It's not just claiming to be trustworthy; it's earning trust daily through transparent communication, kept promises, and decisions that put stakeholder well-being alongside organizational goals.

Appendix I

List of Figures

Appendix J

Resources and Further Reading

To continue your Executive Abundance journey, here are trusted resources and opportunities to deepen your clarity, credibility, consistency, and commitment.

Dr. Mitchell Levy Resources

Training & Support

- Book Dr. Mitchell Levy for a keynote, executive workshop, or leadership retreat focused on Executive Abundance.
- Explore coaching packages to develop your personal CPoP and embed credibility practices.
- Executive Abundance Courses: Short alignment courses for CEOs, boards, and C-Suite leaders focused on operationalizing the EA Framework across leadership teams. Access: https://executiveabundance.com/courses
- Contact Mitchell directly to tailor a learning program for your team or association.

Applied Reflection Tools

- The CPoP Architect™: A guided reflection tool designed to help leaders articulate a clear CPoP (Customer Point of Possibilities) and align their communication and behavior accordingly.
  Access: https://aha.pub/TheCPoPArchitect
- The Credibility Compass™: A reflective framework that helps leaders examine how they show up as Trusted, Known, and Liked across stakeholder groups, with practical guidance for strengthening credibility through behavior.
  Access: https://aha.pub/TheCredibilityCompass

Websites:

- https://MitchellLevy.com
- https://ExecutiveAbundance.com
- https://SocialComplement.com
- https://MitchellLevy.Substack.com

TEDx Talks:

- "We Are Losing Our Humanity, and I'm Tired of Watching It Happen!"
- "Being Seen and Being Heard as a Thought Leader"

Contact info:

- LinkedIn: linkedin.com/in/mitchelllevy
- Email: mitchell.levy@gmail.com
- Phone: (+1) 408-257-3000

Recommended Further Reading

- *The Speed of Trust* by Stephen M.R. Covey
- *Dare to Lead* by Brené Brown
- *Leaders Eat Last* by Simon Sinek
- *The Infinite Game* by Simon Sinek
- *Credibility* by Kouzes & Posner
- *Credibility Nation* by Dr. Mitchell Levy

Your journey toward Executive Abundance does not have to be taken alone; reach out, build connections, and keep growing.